# THE TRUTH ABOUT GIRLS AND BOYS

# THE TRUTH ABOUT
# GIRLS and BOYS

## Challenging Toxic Stereotypes
## About Our Children

### CARYL RIVERS and
### ROSALIND C. BARNETT

Columbia University Press      *New York*

Columbia University Press
*Publishers Since 1893*
New York   Chichester, West Sussex
cup.columbia.edu
Copyright © 2011 Caryl Rivers and Rosalind C. Barnett

Library of Congress Cataloging-in-Publication Data
Rivers, Caryl.
The truth about girls and boys : challenging toxic stereotypes about our children /
    Caryl Rivers and Rosalind C. Barnett.
    p. cm.
Includes bibliographical references and index.
ISBN 978-0-231-15162-7 (cloth : alk. paper) — ISBN 978-0-231-52530-5 (ebook)
1. Sex differences (Psychology) in children. 2. Stereotypes (Social psychology).
3. Child development. 4. Child psychology.  I. Barnett, Rosalind C. II. Title.

BF723.S42R58    2011
155.43—dc23                                    2011021228

Columbia University Press books are printed on permanent and durable acid-free
    paper.
This book is printed on paper with recycled content.
Printed in the United States of America

c 10 9 8 7 6 5 4 3 2 1

To our grandchildren, Victoria Tess, Reuben Nathanael, Lauren, Azalea, and Zuey, who will reap the benefits of growing up in a world in which their individual strengths, not their gender, will shape their futures

# CONTENTS

# THE TRUTH ABOUT GIRLS AND BOYS

# 1 INTRODUCTION

A new biological determinism is sweeping through American society. Old myths about gender differences are being packaged in shiny new bottles and sold to parents and teachers desperate to do the best they can for the children in their care. And the major media—including PBS, *Newsweek*, the *New York Times*, the *Washington Post*, *Parents* magazine, and many others—are uncritically embracing these new-old stereotypes.

From the media, you'd think that there is a scientific consensus that boys and girls are profoundly different from birth, and that these differences have huge consequences for aptitude and performance in such areas as math and verbal abilities, for how the sexes communicate, for the careers for which they should aim, and for the kinds of classrooms they should attend.

As a parent or teacher, you can be forgiven for assuming that all of these beliefs are based on fact; the idea of great differences between boys and girls is the new scientific truth, "proved" by many experts and many studies. This toxic message—which is everywhere today—has real-life consequences. Important new research shows that kids pick up very early—often as early as two years of age—on gender stereotypes, and if parents and teachers don't intervene, kids may get stuck in damaging straitjackets.

The true story is exactly the opposite of the popular narrative. The overwhelming consensus, validated by dozens of researchers using well-designed samples, is that girls and boys are far more alike than different in their cognitive abilities and the differences that do exist are trivial. That's not to say there are no differences between the sexes—indeed there are—but when it comes to the way boys and girls learn and the subjects they are good at, sweeping statements about innate gender differences don't hold up. Human beings have multiple intelligences that defy simple gender pigeonholes.

Unfortunately, the real (and complex) story line is generally missing from the popular media. It is buried in scholarly peer-reviewed journals and articles that seldom see the light of day. The stories that dominate the headlines frequently come from a few "experts" and a few studies that are often deeply flawed. In many cases, the samples are too small, the studies are poorly designed, and the subjects are animals, not people. Moreover, many researchers make wild leaps from small, inconclusive findings to Grand Theories.

Others see conspiracies everywhere—such as American Enterprise Institute scholar Christina Hoff Sommers, who claims in her book of the same title that there is a war against boys and that female teachers are deliberately destroying their male students.

Such arguments are repeatedly debunked by serious scientists, but the story line rolls merrily along. We hear that boys are interested in objects while girls are interested in people, that boys have poor verbal skills and girls can't do math, that boys need to read books about combat and girls need to learn science through cosmetics. (These are opinions actually parroted back to the media by classroom teachers.)

If this were all simply arcane scientific trivia, it might not be dangerous, but such ideas are gaining credence among educators across the country, and new curricula are being designed to cater to the "Boy Brain" or the "Girl Brain." In fact, many school districts are reshaping their educational systems, racing to set up single-sex classrooms on the premise of proclaimed massive gender "differences." In short, educational policy decisions are being based on scant or no scientifically sound data.

Even the most enlightened parents can't help but respond to the unending media messages that boys and girls have such different brains, different ways of reasoning, and different hormones that they might as well belong to separate species. Parents are led to believe that their little girls and boys need different stimulation; they need to be handled differently, educated differently, and given different levels of protection.

Educators, too, fall prey to such ideas. Many teachers are buying books that promote extreme gender differences based on questionable science. At the 2006 National Association of Independent Schools convention (where we were keynote speakers), one teacher told us that his headmaster was redesigning the entire curriculum on the ideas of best-selling author Leonard Sax, who promotes pseudoscientific ideas about boys and girls. Unfortunately, management gurus are also telling young women that they should focus on their communication skills and multitasking abilities, while accepting the "fact" that men have more ability to focus and command.

The New Segregation?

Today, there is a major drive under way to create more gender-segregated public school classrooms. The Bush administration issued new rules in 2006, letting schools override the antidiscrimination provisions of Title IX, thereby clearing the way for many more classrooms segregated by gender. As of January 2010, 547 public schools in the United States offered single-sex classrooms. South Carolina has recently set the goal of having such classrooms widely available. Not surprisingly, then, more school administrators, teachers, and parents are considering this idea carefully. They appear to be buying the notion of great gender differences in cognitive abilities, while the opposing view—backed by the latest peer-reviewed science—gets short shrift.

Increasingly, new public policies, the debate on American education, and the marketing of products to kids are being seen through the "gender lens."

What's on offer is astonishingly retrograde—almost Victorian—in its view of the sexes. In fact, we're going backwards in many areas, with toy stores setting up more and more blue and pink toy aisles.

This message is couched in the language of science, but what's really being offered is at best pseudoscience, in which anecdotes are presented as data and sweeping generalizations are based on inconclusive research.

We hear from one best seller, *The Female Brain*, that such an entity does exist, but the book's own footnotes contradict what the author says. A runaway best seller, *The Dangerous Book for Boys*, urges a return to the boyhood of the rural nineteenth century, when boys skinned rabbits, shot arrows, and reenacted heroic male battle adventures. Girls have no place in this scenario of adventure and risk, but distressingly, Disney films has already bought the rights to the book. Amazon is recommending a new book by best-selling author Michael Gurian, titled *The Minds of Boys*. Among Gurian's unscientific beliefs is the notion that boys have brain structures that girls don't possess, structures that allow boys to excel in math and science. The author is in great demand as a lecturer at schools and education conventions. Meanwhile, the *New Republic* contends that schools offer "verbally drenched" curricula that discriminate against boys, and *New York Times* columnist David Brooks writes that we have to give boys simple books about combat to overcome their lack of verbal ability.

4

At a time when parents, teachers, and the public at large need real information, what they get instead is bias and misinformation, and both boys and girls are being harmed by the simplistic, stereotyped view of their "natures." Stereotypes retain their hold, especially when they are endlessly promoted in advertising, TV, the news media, popular music, movies, novels—everywhere. These powerful beliefs act as funnels, directing girls and boys into particular ways of being and behaving. We are told that girls can't excel at math, and shouldn't aspire to the highest levels of management, and that boys are hyperaggressive, and can't be nurturing or cooperative even if they want to. Children internalize such stereotypes at an early age, thus putting brakes on the fulfillment of their individual potential.

However, research tells us that these stereotypical beliefs have no basis in fact. There is no evidence to support the claims of massive innate gender differences in such critical areas as math, verbal ability, nurturance, aggression, leadership, and self-esteem. Most differences are tiny, a far cry from what the media and some very vocal pundits present.

It's ironic that as neuroscience tells us more and more about the similarity of our brains, popular culture incessantly beams the opposite message, drowning out the real story. Lise Eliot, a professor of neuroscience at the University of Chicago, conducted an exhaustive review of the scientific literature on human brains from childhood to adolescence and concluded that there is "surprisingly little evidence of sex differences in children's brains."

Despite this fact, parents and teachers still operate as if the sexes were hugely different. Eliot notes, "In many ways the world for preschoolers is more gender divided than ever." This trend is troubling because "the more parents hear about hard-wiring and biological programming, the less we bother tempering our pink or blue fantasies and start attributing every skill of deficit to innate sex differences. Your son is a later talker. Don't worry, he's a boy. Your daughter is struggling with math. It's okay, she's very artistic."

The net effect of all this is more, rather than less, stereotyping by parents and teachers, the most important adults in children's lives.

## A Message That Needs to Be Heard

Although we are swimming against this strong media current, our voices are starting to be heard. We were, as we noted, invited to keynote the annual convention of the National Association of Independent Schools in Denver in 2006. Between us, we have been invited to give major presentations at Columbia University and at a major conference on boys and girls sponsored by the American Enterprise Institute. We have presented our ideas at schools around the United States and Canada, and we gave a major keynote lecture in Germany on coeducation and gender stereotypes. Building on our lectures and extensive research, this book has an urgent message. Adults provide the environment for our children. What we do and how we do it affect how our children's brains begin to organize themselves and to process information. We now know that the young brain is not something that is formed at birth and always remains the same. New pathways are constantly being laid down and others are being destroyed.

The good news is that armed with understanding and solid information, we can avoid the traps of fostering traditional—and restrictive—behavior in children. And we can limit the unintended consequences of well-intentioned parents and teachers who may be unwittingly encouraging stereotyped behavior in children.

An example: It may be that mothers in particular have internalized stereotypes about boys, even when their children are very young. Mothers of boys, research finds, often talk differently to their sons than to their daughters. Boys are often given commands and instructions—*"Pick up those blocks!" "Come here!"* while mothers more often infuse emotion into exchanges with their daughters (*"Does the doll feel good today?" "Do you like Michele and her mommy?"*) Young boys may get the message that emotions are not "boy turf."

Here's another example. Every time parents toss a ball around with their sons, the boys' brains learn something about speed, distance, perspective, and velocity. As a boy gets better at this game, he wants to play more, and his parents are likely to want to engage more in ball playing. A daughter who doesn't get such experience doesn't develop these brain pathways and connections, is less good at playing catch, and is less likely to engage with her parents in this kind of activity. Years later, she may decide she's not good at sports—or math.

And while girls in affluent schools that sponsor elite sports, such as varsity soccer, are learning great new spatial and motor skills, girls in poorer public schools are not so fortunate. In such districts, recess is being canceled and girls have many fewer opportunities to take part in sports, in school as well as at home.

Our children face a time of unprecedented change and uncertainty. One thing for sure is that we are moving fast into an information age in which skills such as problem solving, critical thinking, communication, and cooperation will be crucial for success. All our children, boys and girls, need to master these skills, and they all have the ability to do so.

Of course, over time, because of boys' and girls' varying experiences, some gender differences do appear, and they can have consequences for behavior or career choice. But if parents and teachers act early enough to counteract stereotypes, these differences can be overcome.

We will look at the most popular books on parenting that deal with gender, and show how they are filled with pseudoscience. Many best-selling books have a very traditional agenda and are written in a way that makes them seem highly authoritative. But those who read these books don't know how biased and ill-informed they are.

Here are the major problems these books have, to one degree or another:

- They are not written by trained researchers in the field.
- They are based on anecdotal material or on the authors' own observations.
- They are based on studies of adults, not children.
- They are heavily based on animal studies.
- They are based on clinical work with disturbed patients.
- They make sweeping generalizations from small and non-representative samples.
- They are not informed by peer-reviewed scientific data.
- They are often written by people with an ideological agenda, who blithely disregard new science that challenges their entrenched positions and threatens their financial stake in promoting their ideas.

Through the incredible attention given to these books by the media, most of us believe that the sexes are vastly different. And these beliefs affect our expectations for our kids, the experiences we provide for them, our response to their behaviors and choices, the schools we select for them, and just about every other aspect of our relationships with them. They also affect the expectations kids develop about their own competencies.

Harvard's Howard Gardner, one of the nation's most eminent experts on learning, suggests a different way of looking at kids. His thesis is that there are seven different kinds of "intelligences" and that children can possess them all, although they might be most gifted in particular areas. (More detail about this later on.)

Gardner thinks that children, when they are very young, have wide-ranging curiosity and learn all sorts of things from the world around them. "In the first five years of life, young children the world over develop powerful theories and conceptions of how the world works—the physical world and the world of other people. They also develop at least a first-draft level of competence with the basic human symbol systems—language, number, music, two-dimensional depiction, and the like."

The intriguing fact is that kids don't need adults teaching them how to do all this. "Children develop these symbolic skills and these theoretical conceptions largely by dint of their own spontaneous interactions with the world in which they live."

But as this period closes, kids enter the culture created by adults, a culture that guides them into areas the adults think appropriate. Shortly after the age at which school begins, youngsters begin to assume a quite different stance toward the opportunities in their culture. More often than not, these opportunities are highly different for boys and girls. "This period then functions as an apprenticeship—an apprenticeship en route to expertise in specific domains, and an apprenticeship en route to expertise in the ways of one's culture. The free-ranging explorations of the young child have ceased."

It's almost like the Middle Ages, when young children, especially boys, were sent off to guilds to become stonemasons, painters, armor-makers, and so on. (Girls, of course, were mainly confined to the domestic arena.)

At this critical developmental juncture, kids are no longer little sponges soaking up what they find interesting; rather they have become very apt and motivated students of what adults think they ought to know.

If Gardner's ideas are correct, grown-ups have tremendous power over what and how school-age children learn. Instead of having the whole world at their fingertips, school-age children are being directed to certain paths and away from others. And when adults point out a direction, children want to go there.

If we are not careful, we may be cutting off these little eager beavers from the "road not taken," as Robert Frost would have said it. If the authors of this book have a bias, it's that we believe school should encourage children to develop all the intelligences they possess, to find their passion by drinking from many springs. And if schools can't—or won't do that—then parents need to do it.

Our idea is the exact opposite of the gender-lens theories about education that force kids down certain "gender-appropriate" paths. This notion is especially critical today because we shouldn't close off options for any of our children. Nearly all of them will spend the bulk of their adult years involved in the workforce. Flexibility will be the key to whether they succeed or fail in both their economic lives and their personal lives. Satisfaction in both arenas will be vital for their personal fulfillment and well-being.

Today, parents and educators are being fed a diet of junk science that is at best a misunderstanding of the research and at worst what amounts to a deliberate fraud on the American public. The education of our children is too important to the future of our nation to allow this situation to go unchallenged.

To get to the truth about girls and boys, we need to go beyond pink and blue.

# 2   BRAINS IN PINK AND BLUE?

If your young daughter blurted out that she wanted to be a math-ematician—or an architect, or an astronaut—would a rush of fear run up your spine? Would you worry that she would be setting her-self up to fail? Would you believe that, in general, the female brain is just not meant for such pursuits? Would you encourage her, instead, to go into a field where she could work with people, use her caring skills and not have to compete with males, who are more suited by nature for such "non-nurturing" occupations?

Indeed, you might well experience such emotions if you had been reading best-selling books and tracking media narratives in recent years. Currently the idea of "boy and girl brains" is very much in fashion. But the notion that women and men are cognitively differ-ent has old and deep roots.

In the Victorian era, scientists were obsessed with the idea that white men were the proper lords of creation, ideally equipped to lead, make decisions, exert power, and impose their will on every-body else. Women and black males were childlike in comparison. To prove their case, scientists actually packed cadaver brains with lead buckshot and weighed them. Indeed, the white male brains held more pellets than either the white female brains or the black male brains.

Not surprisingly, the scientists reasoned that the greater volume of the white male brains meant that white men were uniquely capable of the higher intellectual functions. Women and black males, in contrast, were likened to children, who were incapable of such higher thinking. As one Parisian scientist decreed in 1879, "There are a large number of women whose brains are closer in size to those of gorillas, than to most developed male brains. This inferiority is so obvious that no one can contest it for a moment, only its degree is worth discussing."[1]

It was discovered years later that brain size is related to overall body size. No wonder the skulls of white males were larger than those of white females; white women are, on average, smaller physically than white men. But what about the black males? As Steven Jay Gould points out in *The Mismeasure of Man*, the scientists often chose for their studies the skulls of Hottentots—a group of blacks that was especially small in stature. So, of course, their smaller skulls held fewer pellets.

The idea that female brains were small—closer to those of children or animals than to those of human males—persisted for generations. In addition, the accepted medical wisdom of the era was that the female brain and ovaries could not develop at the same time, meaning that education would interfere with motherhood. In 1906 the influential psychologist G. Stanley Hall, the president of Clark University, wrote, "Over-activity of the brain during the critical period of the middle and late teens will interfere with the full development of mammary power and of the functions essential for the full transmission of life generally."[2]

Such ideas were enormously powerful—they kept women out of universities, out of professions such as law and medicine, and out of the voting booth. After all, could small-brained females be entrusted with the affairs of the Republic?

As it turned out, the "science" linking education with reduced fertility was completely bogus. No one believes today that female brains and reproductive organs can't develop simultaneously. Moreover, in the 1970s, scientists recalculated the data from the old "pellet" experiments, and the measurements proved to be very inaccurate. Nonetheless, all sorts of discrimination against women and blacks was justified by this "evidence."

With the advent of more-sophisticated technology, researchers were able to reliably correlate brain size with intelligence and other cognitive capacities. The result: there is no relationship between brain size and intelligence. It is clear that measuring the volume of the human skull gives us no insight whatsoever into the dynamic nature of the brain.

## A Step Ahead, a Step Back

In the 1970s the women's movement broke down the gender barriers to medical and law schools, the Supreme Court, the military, and the astronaut corps, to name a few. "Free to Be You and Me" was a mantra that urged parents to see their child's potential, not old gender stereotypes.

But the tide appeared to turn back in the 1990s, as the backlash against women's new roles continued to churn. A veritable cornucopia of books tumbled from publishing houses and sold briskly. They bore titles such as *Why Men Don't Listen and Women Can't Read Maps* (Barbara and Allan Pease),[3] *Boys and Girls Learn Differently* (Michael Gurian, Patricia Henry, and Terry Trueman),[4] *Why Gender Matters* (Leonard Sax),[5] and the granddaddy of them all, *Men Are from Mars and Women Are from Venus*, by John Gray.[6] This über best seller was written by a self-styled family therapist whose degree came from a school closed down by the California attorney general as a diploma mill. Even though it was a down-market, sentimental mess of pseudoscience, for a time it outsold the Bible.

At the same time, new developments in brain imaging were coming on the scene, resulting in a whole new group of studies purporting to show how male and female brains actually functioned. Scientists turned up some intriguing findings that apparently revealed genuine anatomical and functional differences between the sexes.

But how definitive these studies will prove to be, whether they accurately predict aptitudes or performance in any particular area of life, and what can be extrapolated from them about any individual man or woman remain virtually unknown.

As Mark Liberman,[7] professor of linguistics and computer science at the University of Pennsylvania, explains, "It's recently fashionable for books and articles to enlist neuroscience in support of the view that men and women are essentially and unavoidably different, not just in size and shape, but also in just about every aspect of the way they see, hear, feel, talk, listen and think. These works tend to confirm our culture's current stereotypes and prejudices."

Unfortunately, the "difference" theorists take some suggestive findings—a few psychological tests here, some brain scans there, a few studies of monkey behavior here, some research on male and female hormones there—and construct elaborate air castles of theory about what men and women are *really* like and, more dangerously, how they should conduct their lives.

Even scarier, recent evidence[8] finds that college-educated individuals, *even if they have had courses in neuroscience*, are strongly influenced by irrelevant neuroscience language. If such people are unconvinced by your argument, all you have to do to change their minds is to toss some neuroscience jargon into your pitch. No wonder teachers and school administrators are swayed by best-selling books filled with such jargon.

And too often it is jargon, not science, that's offered up to mass audiences. In "the Battle of the Brains," the truth too often is obscured by politics, ideology, and agendas. To understand what we really know about this magnificent organ, we have to look at how the current research got to where it is now.

## Our Fascination with Brains

For the first six weeks in utero, all of us are female. It is only when the fetus begins producing testosterone and other sex-specific hormones that male and female embryos start down different developmental paths. Some claim that these early hormones leave an indelible and critical imprint on the brains of boys and girls that forever shapes their lives. Others disagree.

Perhaps it is no wonder that as the only species that can contemplate our own being, we are enthralled with understanding our brains. How do they work? How do they change over time? What do they tell us about how we learn, communicate, and experience the world? All these are fascinating topics that engage the best efforts of neuroscientists across our country and the world. Yet the only question that seems to dominate the media and public interest is gender differences: Are boys' and girls' brains different?

Before turning to that question, let's take a look at how brain research has evolved over the years. The first point is that our understanding of the brain has been and still is dependent on the techniques we have for assessing the brain.

Early studies were severely limited. Researchers had access only to cadaver brains. What were these early scientists able to study? More crucial, what were they *not* able to study?

One stream of early research, as we've noted, entailed assessing the volume of matter that skulls could hold. The reasoning was that the larger the brain, the more cognitive capacity it had and therefore the better it could process information. Men were really the superior sex. All these speculations were made without the benefit of anyone ever having touched, held, or even seen a human brain. The absence of any knowledge of the brain itself did not stop many medical and other professionals from making sweeping—and very wrong—speculations.

Early researchers were also limited in their understanding of the incredible plasticity of the brain. How could they possibly have known that the brain, through maturing and interacting with external stimuli, is constantly changing? Newer ideas about the highly interactive nature of the brain, about the constant loss and addition of neural pathways in response to what is happening in the body and to environmental stimuli, were not available to early researchers. For example, only recently have we learned about such processes as neuronal pruning and "synaptogenesis," through which neuronal interconnections become more refined. It is easy to understand that without this information, they would have tended to discuss the brain as if it were a static organ, like the spleen. Even today such references are common, despite the fact that ample evidence tells us that the opposite is true. Indeed, references to boys' brains and girls' brains echo the old static picture of this complex organ. Because the brain is ever changing in response to all sorts of learning, the brain of any one boy may differ considerably from that of another boy. And, of course, the same is true for girls.

While some researchers were filling cadaver skulls with lead pellets, others, who had access to recently deceased bodies, were able to examine real brains. One of the first things they noticed was gross anatomical differences between female and male brains. (Of course, they might also have noticed gross anatomical differences between younger and older brains or even between the brains of right- and left-handed people, if they had wanted to look!)

Although we are still at a very early stage of understanding the brain, an array of recently developed technologies has given us new ways to peer into its operations. We can see that there are indeed gender differences in the brain that are primarily structural. But what are we to make of this fact? The big and as yet unanswered question is how structural differences relate to behavior? What real-world effects do they have?

Here's an example of this dilemma. Professor Godfrey Pearlson[9] in the Department of Psychiatry, Behavior Science, and Mental Hygiene at Johns Hopkins University Medical School and director of the Division of Psychiatric Neuroimaging, found that a part of the parietal lobe tends to be larger in male brains than in female ones. This particular area of the brain "is involved in spatial and mathematical reasoning, skills at which boys tend to perform better than girls."

However, merely demonstrating that two events coexist does not prove that one "causes " the other. It might tend to rain every time you leave your umbrella at home, but that does not mean that leaving your umbrella at home is the reason for the rain. And since, as we'll see later in our math chapter, girls have made great leaps in the areas of math and science in a very short time, it's doubtful that one lobe tells the whole story.

Some brain researchers are convinced that the gender differences they have uncovered have functional consequences, even though no such linkages have been established. But most neuroscientists today agree that a major mystery of the brain is the relationship between structure and function.

Lessons from New Technology

After the era of cutting and weighing and the questionable insights gleaned from those techniques, the next major advance in understanding the brain came from the development of magnetic resonance imaging (MRI). MRI is a noninvasive medical test that helps physicians diagnose and treat medical conditions. The patient lies completely still in a special tube-like structure, while pictures of thin sections of the brain are made. These images are generated by using a powerful magnetic field, radio frequency pulses, and a computer. The images can then be examined on a computer monitor, printed, or copied to a CD. Detailed MRI images allow physicians to better evaluate parts of the body and certain diseases that may not be assessed adequately with other imaging methods such as X-ray, ultrasound, or computed tomography (also called CT or CAT scanning).

While vastly more sophisticated than the techniques that preceded it, MRI shares some of the same limitations of earlier techniques, at least from the perspective of understanding how the brain actually functions. For all its advances, MRI generates static images of the brain—it cannot provide any more insights into the dynamism of this highly interactive organ than could the pellets and scales of earlier neuroscientists.

Nevertheless, MRI studies did provide some important information. For example, in 2006, the first report[10] was published exploring the relationship between age and maturation of regions of the brain associated with higher-order language skills. This study was done using a population of "normal" children aged 7–19. (Most studies in the past had been done with children who were "neurologically compromised"—that is, they had a suspected central nervous system pathology.)

To isolate the effects of age on the brain activity of the children, researchers had to first determine whether their results might be influenced by the effect of gender or the interaction of age and gender. They found no statistically significant effects for either. In other words, the linkage between age and the maturation of language and speech areas of the brain is unaffected by gender. According to the researchers, during the period in which youngsters are acquiring language skills, there are no gender differences in neural activity in the language- and speech-producing areas of the brain. (Here, too, the children were at rest, and the data therefore do not shed light on how the brain operates when it is engaged in a task.)

One major new study[11] tracked for the first time the development of brain volume by the age of the child. How quickly, the researchers asked, does the brain reach its maximum volume, at what age does that occur, and are there gender differences in this process? The research found that there are gender differences. Girls' brain volume reaches its maximum size earlier, at 10.5 years, whereas boys reach this marker at 14.5 years.

Does this matter in real life? Maybe yes, maybe no. But the website of the major group that advocates for single-sex public schools, the National Association for Single Sex Public Education (NASSPE), jumped the gun by declaring this finding to be "the key insight from the past five years of neuroscience research in brain development."[12] NASSPE claims that the scientists found no overlap in the trajectories of brain development in girls and boys and takes that as evidence that girls and boys must be taught differently. It asks, "Why is this so important? Here's why. If you teach the same subjects to girls and boys in the same way, then by the age of 12 or 14, you will have girls who think 'geometry is tough' and boys who believe 'art and poetry are for girls.'"

But what's the real story? First, NASSPE got the science wrong by claiming there is no overlap between boys and girls. There is *considerable* overlap, meaning that while the average girl's brain reaches its maximum volume at 10.5 years, a significant proportion of boys' brains also reach their maximum volume at the same age. Knowing a child's gender does not automatically mean you can say at what age his or her brain will be fully developed. Second, the scientists themselves say they have no idea what the academic implications of their findings are—if any.

Rhoshel Lenroot,[13] chair of Infant, Child, and Adolescent Psychiatry at the University of New South Wales, states it clearly: "Our study did not include behavioral data, and so *we could draw no conclusions* [emphasis added] as to how (or if) the structural changes we observed could be related to the maturation of different cognitive abilities." She and her colleagues caution: "Differences in brain size between males and females should not be interpreted as implying any functional advantage or disadvantage."

One of the basic premises of solid science is that you can't generalize beyond what your data tell you. But NASSPE consistently does just that. Because this group is so well funded and so well connected to the media, misinformation suggesting much greater implications of brain data than any reputable scientist would support quickly spreads.

## The Working Brain

The newest tool in the neuroscientist's arsenal holds great promise. Functional magnetic resonance imaging (fMRI) is a procedure that uses MRI to measure the tiny metabolic changes that take place in an active part of the brain. The crucial word here is "active." It is now possible to generate images of the brain that show which areas are actively working while subjects are engaged in performing tasks. A 2007 study[14] using fMRI technology warrants some discussion. In a complicated study of 300 boys and girls, 5–18 years of age, the researchers found some gender differences in the relationship between activity in certain areas of the brain used by children doing a complex task. It required them to listen to stories read to them and then answer questions about the stories. Whereas there were gender differences in the areas of the brain engaged in these activities, "there were no significant differences in performance between the boys and the girls."

Thus, in one of the few studies probing how the brain accomplishes complex language tasks, there is evidence that boys and girls may use different "brain" strategies to accomplish the same tasks—and that they accomplish these tasks equally well. It appears that there is no simple one-to-one relationship between particular areas of the brain and children's performance.

It is also important to remember that areas of the brain children use to perform a task may reflect prior learning rather than innate differences. When the participants are children who are old enough to take part in research studies and provide reliable data, they have already been exposed to massive amounts of learning. They have had countless interactions with their parents, siblings, teachers, friends, with games, books, a variety of media, and so forth. So the ways in which they process information as seen in an fMRI can't be assumed to reflect any "innate" structures. Indeed, to make that assumption is to hark back to the old and outdated notion of the static brain. An fMRI cannot be interpreted as the way the brain processes information independent of whatever developmental or learning situations have occurred.

It may be helpful to think of the brain as a huge transportation hub—a neural Grand Central Station. Speeding trains constantly come and go on different tracks, buses are dispatched to different highways, and people rush to and fro to get to their destinations. It's hard to take in the whole panorama at a glance. The fact that the brain is a constantly changing organ makes the problem of establishing linkages between structures and activity patterns and function especially difficult. Even if gender differences are found in some brain structures, it is not clear that those differences are innate, or a reflection of the tendency for boys and girls to have different socialization experiences, or a bit of both.

Although we've come a long way from the idea that dolls are for girls and blocks are for boys, male and female children often play with different toys, have different learning experiences, and interact differently with their parents and teachers. All this activity undoubtedly shapes their brains.

But there's still a great deal of individuality in this overall picture. What about a girl who loves building block towers, playing video games on computers, and spending hours kicking a soccer ball around? Would her fMRI look more "male-like" than that of a kid who has had a more "girly" childhood? When a child is engaged in a task and a particular area of the brain lights up, how are we to know whether that same area would light up if the child had had a totally different set of prior learning experiences?

It is safe to say that someday techniques for finer-and-finer-grained analyses of the brain and its functions will be developed. For example, one intriguing 2005 study[15] using MRI data found gender differences in the relationship between gray and white matter in the brain and IQ scores. Nevertheless, men and women achieved similar IQ results. What does this mean? Not a lot. The researchers state that "there is no singular underlying neuroanatomical structure to general intelligence and that different types of brain design may manifest equivalent intellectual performance."

Someday we may be able to establish the elusive causal connections between brain structures, activity patterns, and real-world consequences. At that point in time, we may have the appropriate scientific evidence we need to make credible statements about the linkages between gender differences in brain anatomy and meaningful behavioral consequences. Today we are far, far from that enlightened age.

Yet if you look at the major narrative presented by the popular media, you'd think that all these mysteries have been solved. All the complexities that have besieged trained researchers have been eliminated. Popular writers advocate teaching girls the way that girls' brains need to be taught and teaching boys the way that boys' brains need to be taught. These self-proclaimed experts glibly and repeatedly make definitive statements about how schools should be set up and how parents and teachers should behave. Never mind that these "gurus" are not neuroscientists and do not cite supporting peer-reviewed evidence for their claims. Most worrisome, these best-selling authors have the ear of educational policymakers, teachers, and parents. And, as we'll see in the next chapter, the media gobble up their message.

# 3 MORE PINK AND BLUE

Do males "systematize"? Are males naturally attuned to systems and objects, while females are by nature attuned to people and caring? This notion has received widespread—and uncritical—attention in major publications around the world. It has become a "factoid"— one of those pieces of misinformation that gets repeated so many times that people come to accept it as fact even though they have no idea where it comes from. The idea was set out by psychologist Simon Baron-Cohen of Cambridge University in his book *The Essential Difference*.[1] He claims that the male brain is the "systematizing brain," while the female brain is the "empathizing" brain. He has been quoted in the *New York Times,* in a *Newsweek* cover story, in a PBS documentary, and in many other major media outlets. And he is a frequent keynote speaker at important conferences.

What, according to this theory, are the advantages of the male brain? Such brains are ideally suited for leadership and power. Specifically, they are hardwired for mastery of hunting and tracking, trading, achieving and maintaining power, gaining expertise, tolerating solitude, using aggression, and taking on leadership roles.

And what of the female brain? It is specialized for four functions: making friends, mothering, gossip, and "reading" a partner. In this scenario, girls' and women's brains are built for "empathizing"— identifying another person's emotions and responding with appropriate emotion. Girls and women are so focused on others that they have little interest in figuring out how the world works, or any of the other activities that presumably occupy the male brain. As a result, these are the jobs that Baron-Cohen suggests for women: "counselors, primary school teachers, nurses, carers, therapists, social workers, mediators, group facilitators or personnel staff." Note that these are largely low-paid female ghetto jobs with little power.

But where does this theory come from? On what evidence should we tell girls to aim for jobs that too often avoid understanding systems, developing managerial talent, or aiming for high achievement and leadership? Surely such a prescription should be the result of carefully collected data.

In fact, this whole notion is based on a single study, done in Baron-Cohen's lab, of day-old infants. It purports to show that day-old baby boys look longer at mobiles while day-old baby girls look longer at human faces. From this tiny seed grew a much-quoted theory of highly gendered brains.

But the study had major problems. First of all, it was an "outlier" study. No one else has replicated these findings, including Baron-Cohen himself. In fact, this study is so flawed as to be almost meaningless, says cognitive psychologist and infant cognition expert Elizabeth Spelke,[2] codirector of Harvard's Mind/Brain/Behavior Interfaculty Initiative.

Why? For these reasons:

• The experiment lacked crucial controls against experimenter bias and was not well designed. Female and male infants were propped up in a parent's lap and shown, side by side, an active person and an inanimate object. Since newborns can't hold their heads up independently, their visual preferences could well have been determined by the way their parents held them.

• There is a large body of literature that flat-out contradicts Baron-Cohen's study, providing evidence that male and female infants tend to respond equally to people and objects. Better-designed studies show no male superiority in spatial and mathematics abilities at an early age.

• As Spelke notes of Baron-Cohen's work, "This is one single isolated experiment. Its findings fly in the face of dozens of studies on similar aspects of cognition carried out on young babies over decades. It is astonishing how much this one study has been cited, when the many studies that show no difference between the sexes, or difference in the other direction, are ignored."

Some studies, in fact, show that female babies understand, before boy babies do, that the distance an object travels depends on the force with which it is hit. Female infants pass this milestone at 5.5 months and males at 6.5 months. But where are the headlines that announce "Females Have Advantage in Mathematical Reasoning"? They don't exist.

The way in which very flawed information gets into the media pipeline—and ultimately into the minds of parents, teachers, and policymakers—is illustrated by this statement from *Parents* magazine[3] in June 2007: "Girls prefer dolls [to blocks and toys] because girls pay more attention to people while boys are more enthralled with mechanical objects."

Obviously the magazine is channeling Baron-Cohen, presenting his questionable theory as fact, never mentioning the overwhelming evidence that contradicts it. One can imagine parents, after reading this story, declining to buy blocks for their daughter because they conclude that she is just not naturally interested in them. Preschool teachers might not intervene when boys monopolize the block corner, keeping the girls from building castles or bridges. Since we know that block play is very helpful in enhancing spatial concepts, these parents and teachers—thinking they are doing what's best for children—are in fact denying girls valuable learning experiences.

## The Feeling Brain?

Many people just can't stop trying to argue that something about girls' and women's brains makes them the "feeling" sex. And, conversely, that male brains are just not up to snuff in this department. Baron-Cohen insists that not only are females bad at systematizing, but their brains are totally geared to emotion.

Empathizing females are expected to pick up on what others are obviously feeling, but in addition, according to Baron-Cohen, they are hardwired to respond to "any emotion or state of mind, not just the more obvious ones, such as pain." Any other person's emotion—whether he or she is close to you or distant—triggers empathy in the "natural" woman. Describing this mechanism, he says, "Imagine that you not only see Jane's pain but you also automatically feel concern, wince, and feel a desire to run across and help alleviate her pain." Would any woman so fully occupied with caring for everybody around her have the ability to lead others? Hardly. She'd barely have the time or the energy to get dressed in the morning. She would also be a prime candidate for depression and burnout.

But at the same time that the mass media were promoting this narrative of über-empathy, a conflicting narrative was grabbing attention. "Mean girls," who bully, taunt, and humiliate their peers, were the subject of best sellers, magazine covers, and even a feature film starring teen idol Lindsay Lohan. How these rotten teens managed to be so loathsome to other girls despite their hardwired, caring brains is something of a mystery. But consistency is rarely a feature of the popular media, which seem relentless in the search for the relationship-obsessed female.

For example, *Parents* magazine in March 2006[4] claimed that girls and women use both sides of their brain more symmetrically than do boys and men. The larger corpus callosum in women explains female intuition and ability to "multitask" and tune in to emotions, the magazine told its readers. (The corpus callosum, or the CC, is the bundle of nerve fibers connecting the left and right brain hemispheres.) The corpus callosum has been getting special attention as far back as the early 1900s, when brain researchers were first able to cut into brains and weigh and measure various sections. But the recent debate was fueled by a 1982 *Science* article about the CC that claimed to be the first report of a reliable sex difference in human brain morphology.[5] *Time*[6] magazine reported in 1992 about the corpus callosum: "Often wider in the brains of women than in those of men, it may allow for greater cross-talk between the hemispheres—possibly the basis for woman's intuition." Although there was some debate at the time, a consensus seemed to suggest that the CC was thicker and larger in women.

The media simply ram amok with this idea. A *Newsweek*[7] cover story ("Why Men and Women Think Differently") suggested that brain differences in the CC might explain "women's intuition." A *New York Times* science editor[8] said this difference discredited "some feminist ideologues" who claimed that women could be as good as men in math if they weren't discouraged in school. *Elle* magazine decreed that the CC was the reason girls do not like physics. Surf the Internet and you will find scores of articles claiming a causal link between female emotion and the corpus callosum. This is another area where journalists too often simply present a very speculative idea as settled science.

But what is the truth? Should boys just withdraw from the arena of emotion, since their brains are clearly not up to it?

In fact, all of the above claims are simply untrue, according to peer-reviewed science:

• *Neuroscience and Biobehavioral Review*[9] (1997) says: "There were no statistically significant corpus callosum area differences between groups." Recent studies using MRI and other methods for studying living human brains, and taking into account such things as differences in brain size, do not support the conventional wisdom that the corpus callosum differs in men and women

• Also, a meta-analysis (a combination of many studies) of 49 studies published since 1989 reveals no significant sex differences in the size or shape of the splenium of the corpus callosum, whether or not an appropriate adjustment is made for brain size.[10]

As Lise Eliot[11] notes in *Pink Brain, Blue Brain*, real data don't matter if educators and psychologists can find some nugget somewhere that confirms their preexisting theories. "So you can still find Michael Gurian and Leonard Sax talking about the corpus callosum, in relation to differences between boys' and girls' learning. For the record: the corpus callosum does not differ between boys and girls."

The truth is that girls' and women's brains don't give them any particular advantage in qualities of empathy, understanding, or compassion, despite many statements to the contrary. *Parents* magazine[12] writes: "Girls' brains are bigger in an area that interprets events and triggers complicated feelings like sadness or empathy— that may be why girls get upset at situations that won't faze a boy." This statement, of course, is logically flawed, since it confuses correlation and causation. Even if it were true that girls had a larger brain area, there's no evidence that such a difference in size would have any consequences for real-world behavior.

Louann Brizendine,[13] best-selling author of *The Female Brain*, says, "A woman knows what people are feeling, while a man can't spot an emotion unless somebody cries or threatens bodily harm."

The idea of boys as emotional basket cases is widely accepted, but it's a factoid, not a fact. The overwhelming evidence from studies of empathy finds no differences between males and females. And even if boys sometimes lag behind, they do catch up. Dr. David Skuse,[14] professor of behavioral and brain sciences at London's Institute of Child Health, reported in 2005 that new research casts doubt on the notion that girls have a large advantage over boys in personal relationships. Describing his study of differences in social intelligence between boys and girls, Skuse said that if girls were hardwired mainly for relationships, they should be significantly better than boys at recognizing emotion. And, at the age of 6, girls indeed were better than boys in this area. But by late adolescence, boys had closed the gap and were very similar to girls. By age 17, the overlap between the sexes in the ability to recognize emotion was better than 90 percent. Other studies show little difference between the sexes in this area at all ages.

What's really intriguing is that when you ask girls and women which sex is the most caring, they say females are. Boys and men say the same thing. "Self-report" studies—where you ask people what they think—are the only ones in which a large gender gap emerges. Everybody agrees with the stereotype. But the overwhelming preponderance of peer-reviewed studies tells a completely different story. When empathy is measured either physiologically or by unobtrusive observations of nonverbal reactions to another's emotional state, no sex differences are evident.[15] In other words, girls have no natural edge in caring or empathy. Why do people believe they do? The authors of one major review of the scientific literature say that it's because nestled inside their heads are ideas about what boys and girls are supposed to be like rather than how they actually behave.

Differences do emerge in how boys and girls respond to situations in which empathy is evoked. For example, when both sexes are exposed to the cries of a baby, girls are more likely than boys to go to the baby and try to comfort it; boys are more reticent. Research tells us that both sexes are equally responsive to the cries, but social learning, not brain differences, shapes their gendered responses.

Thus, if we were to watch the different responses of boys and girls we might conclude that boys were less empathic; we might even conclude that such differences were hardwired. But we would be wrong. We would be misidentifying a learned behavior as an innate behavior.

As for the idea that the corpus callosum is the source of women's intuition, the late psychoanalyst Jean Baker Miller[16] had a better idea.

She explained such intuition as the result of many years of practice among women at observing and understanding the moods and wishes of more-powerful males. This idea was validated by an experiment by psychologist Sara Snodgrass[17] in which men and women were paired and one was randomly assigned the role of boss, the other the role of subordinate. The "subordinate" paid more attention to the "boss," listened harder, and knew more about the boss, whether that person was male or female. Women's intuition, suggested Snodgrass, may really be "subordinate's intuition."

## Weird Science

Parents and teachers need to be very wary of what the media present as "science," especially in popular parenting magazines, which too rarely explain complex studies. Small samples abound in the difficult area of brain research; the numbers are too small to tell us anything definitive, but they may suggest areas of promising research. In the mass media, however, these tiny—and preliminary—studies get easily blown out of proportion.

A classic example: Researchers at Stanford[18] used a brain scanner to see how 12 men and 12 women responded to photographs. Three weeks later, the women remembered events that had an emotional connotation better than the men did. A study of 24 people can't tell us much of anything—especially about such a complex subject as emotion. Nonetheless, a London newspaper[19] soon reported that male brains "are just not built to recall things that women find easy to remember . . . such as a row with their boyfriend."

Shortly thereafter, Maureen Dowd,[20] of the *New York Times*, used the study as the launching pad for a column in which she noted: "Women subjects who participated in the new study got more upset, for longer, than male subjects after being shown pictures of dead bodies, gravestones, crying people and dirty toilets." The average reader was left with the "fact" that women's brains are wired to be better at emotions. But even if such findings hold up in studies with larger samples, there's another, more reasonable explanation: In our culture, women are usually the ones in charge of managing the emotional lives of their families, and that could be why emotional issues trigger recall. Does a woman remember the birthday of her mother-in-law because her brain is wired for emotion? Or because it's her job to buy the present?

### Miserable Achievers?

"Is chemistry destiny?" *New York Times* columnist David Brooks[21] recently asked. His answer was a resounding vote in favor of sheer biological determinism and traditional female roles. He blithely jettisoned a century's worth of research to chirp that "happiness seems to consist of living in harmony with the patterns that nature and evolution laid down long, long ago."

Long, long ago, of course, was when men were in charge of the world and women knew their place, not wanting to vote, attend universities, or venture into politics.

Brooks was citing Brizendine's *The Female Brain*.[22] The book got the kind of media hype that most authors only dream of—interviews on most of the morning network TV shows, interviews on *20/20* and CNN, features in the *New York Times* magazine, the *Washington Post*, the *Chicago Tribune*, *Oprah* magazine—the list goes on and on.

The book claims that the female brain is wired for connection, the same argument offered by Baron-Cohen. But once again, the author (a neuropsychiatrist at the University of California, San Francisco) unfortunately makes huge, unsubstantiated leaps. Take, for example, this statement: "Studies indicate that girls are motivated—on a molecular and a neurological level—to ease and even prevent social conflict."

But as Robin Marantz Henig[23] points out in her excellent *New York Times* review, the data for that statement are "quite fuzzy." The endnote lists nine scholarly articles, with no further explanation given. "From articles (which the reader has to look for in the bibliography), we can surmise that one study was on female mice, one on male and female rats, one (apparently) on female rhesus monkeys, and the other six on humans. But only one of those human studies explicitly mentions 'sex differences' in the title."

You find this sort of sleight of hand in many books and articles that claim science "proves" great gender differences. Rats, cats, and female monkeys may be interesting subjects, but to extrapolate to human behavior from studies about them is like trying to leap the Grand Canyon is a single bound.

If females are hardwired to ease or prevent social conflict, then women should be the peacemakers in all domestic disputes. But researcher Murray Strauss[24] at the University of New Hampshire reports that in studies of family violence, men and women initiate violence in roughly equal numbers. More women than men are injured in such confrontations; when it comes to sheer physical violence, men still have the edge. Females also tend toward "relational" violence, relying on scorn, taunts, and insults. One University of Minnesota study found that a significant number of girls in the fourth through sixth grades were "relationally victimized."[25] A Finnish study of adolescent aggression that included relational aggression concluded, "The claim that human males are more aggressive than females appears to be false."[26]

And while men are far more likely to engage in the kind of violence that lands you in jail, female crime—including violent crime—is rising dramatically all across the world.

But such facts do not deter some popular writers, who still see "sugar and spice" as the universal narrative for all girls. Michael Gurian, a family therapist, is another author who aggressively peddles the idea that girls are hardwired for relationships, and warns that too much achievement will make girls unhappy. Gurian, the best-selling author of twenty books, including *The Wonder of Boys*[27] and *The Wonder of Girls*,[28] runs an institute advocating for the proposition that boys and girls are neurobiologically so different from each other that both sexes require their own separate, gender-tailored educational programs.

Steven Rhoads, a political scientist at the University of Virginia, quotes Gurian at length in *Taking Sex Differences Seriously* (2003).[29] Rhoads also marshals every study he can find—both genuine science and junk science—along with a generous mix of anecdotes, conjectures, and opinions that fit his pre-drawn thesis, to conclude that traditional sex roles provide exactly what both sexes want. If women deny their inborn nature, he says, they will experience "heart-breaking torment." The book has become a hit on the right-wing media circuit (Dr. Laura has called it a "fabulous book").

Like Baron-Cohen, Michael Gurian is quoted widely in the media and appears often on TV and radio as a gender expert. A Lexis-Nexis search shows more than 300 references in major U.S. newspapers to Gurian, who modestly dubs himself "the world's foremost authority in male-female brain differences" on his website. Though he has no formal background in neuroscience—his degree is in journalism—he lectures and also trains and consults with school districts, social agencies, and businesses all over the country on what he calls his "nature-based theory" of biological male-female distinctions. These mainly determine how men and women behave, learn, relate to other people, and work, he claims. Gurian presents as irrefutable scientific "fact" the idea that females "are less able to separate emotion from reason." And he is adamant in insisting that if girls don't focus on relationships, they are heading for unhappiness.

Reading all this, a parent might well ask, If I encourage my daughter in school, will I be starting her down a path that will lead her to misery, spinsterhood, and betrayal of her womanhood? Is achievement toxic for girls?

That is indeed what Gurian asserts. He states categorically that females are driven by hormones and by what he calls "the intimacy imperative" and "the mothering season." He writes that feminism is inherently hostile to men and sets women up as victims of masculinity. He claims that girls are hardwired to want to be wives and mothers. Most girls' highest aspiration is to master intimacy and attachment, not to achieve, he writes.

Gurian argues that if you know your daughter's biological makeup and how her brain functions, you'll understand her soul. Girls need attachment among family and friends above all else. (Traditional) Mom must remain the role model for her daughter, and Dad should stick to being "the hero of her childhood."

As critic Laurie Edwards[30] notes, "Combining questionable science, right-wing sociology, and heavy doses of psychobabble, he finds a 'nature-based' means of justifying the placing of women in a position, not of subservience exactly, but rather of comfortable tradition—a place for which he says they are biologically suited. You know in the first ten pages what you're getting here, and what you're getting ain't pretty."

When Gurian lectured at a national teachers' meeting in Canada, one school board staffer was horrified, saying he was simply spouting "voodoo science."[31] In one of his books Gurian claims that the soul is made of light, and says that fact can be verified, a very peculiar statement for someone who claims to base his work on science.

Still, parents and teachers may be especially susceptible to Gurian's arguments, because they hear similar ones from many quarters. Take the headlines that appeared all over the country in 2005, suggesting that "science" had discovered that men do not like successful women: the *Chicago Sun Times*[32] titled its article "They're Too Smart for These Guys," the *Toronto Star*[33] asked "Are Men Insecure or Are They Merely Intimidated?" and the *New York Times*[34] proclaimed that there were "Glass Ceilings at Altar as Well as Boardroom. The *Atlantic*[35] asked "Too Smart to Marry?" *New York Times* columnist Maureen Dowd lamented that science proves that men don't like achieving women.[36]

As it turned out, the headlines were based on two problematic studies. One of them, conducted by investigators at four British universities (Edinburgh, Glasgow, Bristol, and Aberdeen),[37] found that for every 15-point increase in IQ score above the average, women's likelihood of marrying fell by almost 60 percent.

Really bad news for bright women, right?

*Not.* Neither Dowd nor the *Atlantic* bothered to mention—apparently they did not know—that the data were gathered from men and women born in 1921; the women are all now in their eighties. The very old study has no relevance for today's girls or women. At the time when these bright women were of marriageable age—the 1940s—the institution of marriage was so constraining that they may well have opted for a career instead of the house-bound servitude that marriage would have entailed.

The second study (2004), by researchers at the University of Michigan and UCLA,[38] used a small sample of 120 male and 208 female undergraduates, mainly freshmen. The males rated the desirability as a dating or marriage partner of a fictitious female, described as either an immediate supervisor, a peer, or an assistant.

Surprise, surprise! The freshman males preferred the subordinate over the peer and over the supervisor when it came to dating and mating.

The study, however, was no barometer of adult male preferences. Rather, it reflected teen boys' ambivalence about strong women.

The fact is that men today do not reject high-achieving women. From ages 36 to 40, female high achievers are more likely than other female workers to be married and have kids. Gurian's major argument—that girls will grow up to be unhappy if they pay too much attention to achievement—is simply false. The opposite is true. For example:

• In our major study of adult women,[39] directed by Dr. Barnett and funded by the National Science Foundation, the women highest in well-being were married women with children who worked in high-prestige jobs.

• Sociologist Valerie Oppenheimer,[40] of UCLA, reports that today men are choosing as mates women who have completed their education. The more education a woman has, the more marriageable she is. Unlike the single, unpublished study of college freshmen that got so much media play, this finding comes from an analysis of 80 peer-reviewed studies.

• Heather Boushey,[41] of the Center for Economic Policy Research, found that women between the ages of 28 and 35 who work full-time and earn more than $55,000 per year or have a graduate or professional degree are just as likely to be successfully married as other working women.

• One longitudinal study of 500 couples by the University of Wisconsin–Madison's Janet Hyde[42] found that women who had the highest sexual satisfaction were those who worked and experienced high rewards from their jobs. A good job, it seems, is good for your sex life.

• A 2005 study of 1,053 mothers found that children of working mothers do not suffer socially or intellectually if their mothers work outside the home.[43]

Maybe, just maybe, we should all be worrying in the opposite direction. Maybe it is lack of ambition that will really do our daughters in as far as their happiness goes. Think about this: Many girls who are teenagers today will live to be 90 or even 100 years old; men's wages have been stagnant or declining for thirty years; the divorce rate, while it has dipped somewhat, still hovers around 40 percent; women consistently enter retirement with about half as much money as men do. Unless your dream for your daughter is that she winds up as a bag lady, the anti-ambition story line is a sucker's bet.

## Different Reasoning?

Do girls and boys think in entirely different ways? Some popular writers claim that they do. Michael Gurian says that brain-based research shows that "boys tend to be deductive in their conceptualizations, starting their reasoning process frequently from a general principle and applying it, or ancillary principles, to individual cases." In contrast, girls "tend to favor inductive thinking. They tend to begin with concrete examples in developing a general theory." As a result of their "female style" of thinking, Gurian claims, girls and women are "less able to separate emotion from reason" and "tend to accept emotive intuition as equally valid."

This claim is echoed in *Women's Ways of Knowing*.[44] The authors argue that men value excellence and mastery in intellectual matters and evaluate arguments in terms of logic and evidence. Women, in contrast, are spiritual, relational, inclusive, and credulous.

The notion that women can't separate emotion from reason is an ancient one, and female emotion is especially threatening. Since biblical times, man has been identified with the higher flights of reason, woman with messy, emotional nature. As critic Vivian Gornick[45] writes, "Onto woman is projected all that is worst in man's view of himself, all that is primitive, immature and degrading."

"Woman is less under the influence of the brain than of the uterine system," wrote the prominent physician J. G. Mulligan[46] in 1848. That sentiment was echoed in 1970 by another well-known physician of his day, Dr. Edgar Berman, who said flatly that women were unfit for political office because of their hormones and their unstable natures. When Congresswoman Patsy Mink (D-Hawaii) angrily challenged him, the doctor said it was just her hormones raging out of control.

Today, the same ideas are cast in a more flattering light. Women's hormones aren't raging anymore—it's just that women are choosing to be more domestic, less ambitious, happily conforming to David Brooks' ideas of "natural" patterns. Being rational, after all, isn't so important if you can be so engagingly connected to people, so emotional—so wonderfully . . . democratic.

Is there any truth to these ideas? Do women have a problem with reason? Do girls' and women's brains (and their hormones) compel them to think in a completely different way from men? Is it true, as Michael Gurian claims, that boys are abstract thinkers, and therefore naturally good at things like philosophy and engineering? Girls, on the other hand, are concrete thinkers and do better in math and science if teachers give them objects they can touch, such as beans or buttons to illustrate the lesson.

This is nonsense. One major review[47] of 180 peer-reviewed studies found that "overall, there is no evidence for any form of advanced cognition that is common among men but rare in women, or vice versa. Correspondingly, there is little support for theories postulating qualitatively distinct pathways of cognitive development for females and males."

When we asked Professor Diane Halpern,[48] a leading authority on gender differences in critical thinking and past president of the American Psychological Association, to comment on Gurian's claim that boys tend to be deductive whereas girls tend to be inductive in their thinking, this is what she said: "I doubt that his generalizations are accurate. In fact, I have data on thousands of students, which I have not yet published, that finds no sex differences on these types of thinking skills."

Democratic Brains?

What about the notion that girls' and women's brains actually make them better leaders than men, because they use their supposedly "democratic" leadership style and their ability to communicate to make employees feel good about themselves? Men and boys, in this view, are stuck with the old kick-butt, command-and-control styles of leading.

True? No. The most effective manager, it's now believed, is the "transformational" leader, an innovative role model who gains the trust and confidence of followers, empowering them to reach their full potential. Psychologist Alice Eagly,[49] of Northwestern University, and her colleagues, in a meta-analysis, found that women managers were more "transformational" than men. But the difference was small: 52.5 percent of females and 47.5 percent of males. Both sexes, it seems, are capable of leadership that enables employees to reach their full potential. Putting people into cookie-cutter stereotypes is unscientific and unsophisticated, no matter who is doing it. The fact is, there is so much overlap between the sexes on leadership, nurturance, aggression, communication, and so on that gender is a very poor predictor of such behaviors.

What parents, teachers, and policymakers need to keep in mind when it comes to brain research is that it is all in very early stages, and today's speculations may be tomorrow's disregarded trash. The reemerging "difference" ideology is perhaps most pernicious when it comes cloaked in the academic terms of scientific or scholarly research, making it all sound deeply embedded in objective reality. But it is not. To make the breathtaking leap from a mixed and often speculative body of lab studies to the conclusion that men are equipped by their brains to make better pilots, engineers, and mathematicians and women to make better nurses, child-tenders, and caretakers is beyond absurd. It certainly goes against the grain of what males and females are actually doing in today's world. It also flies in the face of a great deal of solid behavioral science research.

Lise Eliot reminds us in *Pink Brain, Blue Brain* that the brain is constantly changing throughout our lives. "Plasticity is the basis of all learning. And in childhood, the brain is far more plastic, or malleable, than it is at any later stage of life—wiring itself in large measure according to the experiences in which it is immersed from prenatal life through adolescence. . . . Simply put, the brain is what you do with it. Learning and practice rewire the human brain . . . in response to nature or nurture."

The brain is making new connections all through our lives. Our choices—and those that are made for us, especially when we are children—shape our destiny. No static, innate tangle of neurons does it.

In fact, childhood is the time when the brain is most malleable and able to learn and change. This is the worst time to expose people to stereotyped ideas. Lise Eliot points out, "There's enormous danger in this exaggeration of sex difference, first and foremost in the expectations it creates among parents, teachers, and children themselves. Kids rise or fall according to what we believe about them, and the more we dwell on the differences between boys and girls, the likelier such stereotypes are to crystallize into children's self-perceptions and self-fulfilling prophecies" (15).

Since the brain is the slowest-growing organ in the human body, there is time in childhood for outside forces to make a big impact on its development, for good or ill.

This puts more of a burden on parents and teachers to treat each child as an individual and to avoid falling prey to people who peddle what amounts to scientific snake oil. Eliot warns, "Even teachers are now preaching the gospel of sex differences goaded on by bad in-service seminars, by so-called brain-based learning theories, and, perhaps by the chance to excuse their own lack of success with one or the other gender, usually boys.

. . . The new focus on nature seems to be encouraging parents to indulge sex differences even more avidly."

Parents may unknowingly be sabotaging their children's futures. Eliot finds that the more similar boys' and girls' activities are, the more similar their brains will be. And that's a desirable outcome in a world that more and more requires skills and abilities associated with both sexes

The notion of "hardwired" pink and blue brains that inevitably put girls and boys on different paths makes for a catchy headline or a titillating sound bite, but as science it definitely rates an F.

Indeed, we may discover some structural differences in the brains of men and women; in some tests, different parts of men's and women's brains light up under positron-emission tomography (PET) scans when they are performing similar tasks. But the simple fact of a structural difference means nothing unless it can be proved that such a difference has some real consequence. Remember, we thought for years that a very real structural difference—men's greater brain size—was important to human intelligence—and it turned out to be of very little consequence.

"There does appear to be more than one brain design," notes Richard Haier,[50] professor of psychology at the University of California, Irvine, whose own studies have shown that women possess, on average, a greater density of white matter, whereas men have more gray matter (gray is the cell bodies of neurons; white is the stuff that connects them). But it is equally interesting, Haier says, that male and female brains arrive at the same destination. IQ scores are essentially equal between the sexes.

# 4 MATH WARS

Lawrence Summers, the former president of Harvard, set off a fire-storm in 2005 when he suggested that the "innate" aptitude of women was a factor behind their low numbers in the top jobs in the sciences and engineering. In other words, girls just don't have the right stuff to compete successfully with high-achieving males.

Both male and female academics complained loudly that Summers was shooting from the hip and drawing very simplistic (if not dead wrong) conclusions from complicated research. As biologist Marlene Zuk[1] of the University of California, Riverside told the *Boston Globe*, Summers had trotted out "the same old lines we've heard for decades—if not for centuries—and they just aren't supported by good data."

To his credit, Summers later made a public apology and said he indeed had the scientific facts wrong. But how many people will remember only the initial headlines, not the critique and the apology? How many school advisors will keep on telling female students not to bother taking tough math courses, and how many parents will steer their daughters toward careers in other fields?

Summers resisted any temptation to hunker down and lash out at critics who took him to task for suggesting that women might be inherently inferior to men at math. Instead, he announced new initiatives at the university for women in math and science.

But many others are playing the "PC" card, saying that critics of Summers' remarks are interfering with legitimate scientific inquiry. We fear that the myth of a female handicap is building—echoed by people who simply don't understand the science. Will the new conventional wisdom be that girls and women really *are* inferior to males at math, but political correctness is being used to obscure that truth?

We are still hearing, over and over again, that Larry Summers was right about girls, math, and science. In a column distributed by the *Washington Post* in 2007, Kathleen Parker[2] writes that Summers "was driven out of his university post in 2005 after he suggested at a conference that gender differences might account for an underrepresentation by women in science, math and engineering. Never mind that scientific evidence suggests as much."

Note that Parker conveniently neglects to mention that Summers *himself* admitted that he got the science wrong

Another myth that surfaced in the wake of the Harvard flap is that we need more research to prove whether or not women are inferior at math. Too many reporters parroted this idea. Sally Quinn,[3] in a column in the *Washington Post*, obviously didn't bother to do her own research when she wrote, "Why don't female mathematicians and scientists, especially at Harvard, get together and research this issue until they have definitive answers instead of reaching for the smelling salts." (Guess what, Sally? They already have.) Writing about the controversy, syndicated columnist George Will[4] said, "There is a vast and growing scientific literature on possible gender differences in cognition. Only hysterics denounce interest in these possible differences." The *Financial Times*,[5] in an editorial, said that Summers launched a "long overdue debate on an issue often judged too sensitive to discuss."

But this particular debate has been going on for more than four decades. Many other articles simply made the assumption that the issue of gender differences in math had not been studied before and that Summers was to be applauded for launching new research. Nothing could be further from the truth, which would have been apparent if some journalists had bothered doing adequate research themselves. There's plenty of evidence on the subject, dating back for many years, nearly all of it showing very small differences in cognitive abilities between the sexes. And brand-new research is proving Summers wrong.

But will the legend of female math inferiority trickle down to parents who want the best futures for their daughters, just as old stereotypes about women and girls proved so resilient in the past?

To avoid that dismal outcome, parents need to know the truth about girls, boys, and math. Here are some of the arguments still being advanced about why girls are not good at math:

- They don't have a "math gene" that boys have.
- They don't have logical brains that systematize.
- They don't score well on the math SAT.
- Boys' hormones kick in at puberty and give them a math advantage.
- Females didn't hunt in prehistory, so girls aren't "hardwired' for spatial abilities.
- Girls just don't like math and science, preferring other subjects.

## The Math Gene

Just maybe, one of the reasons that the president of Harvard had it in his head that girls aren't innately good at math and science may have been the notion of a "math gene" that males supposedly possess and females don't. The idea got such massive publicity that it still hovers around our cultural zeitgeist. In fact, we know that there is no gene for math, just as there is no gene for religious faith, for writing ability, or for any other complex trait. The belief in girls' lack of math ability has been around for a long time, but it was only in the early 1980s that scientists first suggested an actual genetic basis for this defect.

A team of scientists from Johns Hopkins University examined the math SAT tests of 9,927 gifted seventh and eighth graders. The boys outperformed the girls on the test, which prompted the researchers to draw a startling conclusion. Since the children shared the same classrooms, their experiences must have been the same. Therefore, the difference could not be due to environmental factors. It had to be genetic. The researchers suggested that perhaps girls shouldn't even *try* to succeed at math. Their plight was compared to that of a short boy thinking he could make the basketball team.

The influential journal *Science*[6] published the study under the headline "Math and Sex: Are Girls Born with Less Ability?" The mainstream media picked up the cry. The *New York Times*[7] asked, "Are Boys Better at Math?" *Time* looked at "The Gender Factor in Math."[8] The study became a major national story, and many parents worried that their daughters would not be able to compete with their male peers in math. Sadly, some even started to look at their daughters differently. One longitudinal study about ten years later reported that mothers who knew about the articles lowered their expectations of their daughters' math capabilities. One mother remembers breathing a sigh of relief when her daughter nearly flunked chemistry; she was glad that her daughter wouldn't have to compete in that arena. She herself had performed well on math and science on her college boards, but thought that her scores were a fluke.

The "math gene" is another wave in the ocean of flawed ideas about gender that have long been flooding the mass media and the popular imagination. Soon after the first headlines appeared, one of the earliest talking Barbie dolls burbled, "Math class is hard!"

Lost in the maelstrom was the quieter voice of reason. "Just because seventh-grade boys sat the same number of hours in the same classroom doesn't mean they got the same mathematical education," noted Alice Schaffer of Wellesley College, chair of the Women in Math Committee of the American Mathematical Society.[9] Indeed, as it turned out, the kids who took the test showed marked differences in their attitudes about—and experiences with—math. When another Hopkins scientist[10] interviewed the same group of students, she found that the parents of gifted boys picked up on their sons' talents at an early age, bought them math books, and talked with them about their future careers. The parents of gifted girls took little notice of their ability. (That trend, alas, continues, as we'll note later.)

Furthermore, in the Hopkins study, Asian males consistently outscored Caucasian males. Why did no one propose an Asian male math gene? Too scary for white guys? Also (notes psychologist Virginia Valian[11] of Hunter College), in tests that compared grammar-school kids in the United States, Taiwan, and Japan, Asian girls score almost twice as high as American boys. (An Asian *girl* gene?) This fact is rarely reported in the American media.

## Systematizing Brains

We thoroughly debunked this idea in the previous chapter, but people keep repeating the same old phrases, like a broken record. Michael Gurian[12] told an education conference in Canada that no more than 20 percent of girls could aspire to be engineers or architects, and that women lack natural technical ability. He says that only girls with brains that work like boys' brains can understand spatial concepts such as math and science. He claims that the structure of most girls' minds makes it too hard for them to grasp subjects like calculus and physics. Does this idea sound bizarre? Indeed. But a news report on the Canadian conference said that teachers were "lining up" to buy his books. The *Chicago Tribune*,[13] in an article that often cites his theories as if they were fact, says his books have won "universal praise." As we said earlier, there is simply no good evidence that the structure of girls' brains makes them unfit for math and science. In fact, Elizabeth Spelke[14] of Harvard identifies five "core systems" as the foundations of mathematical reasoning.

First, a system for representing small exact numbers of objects—the difference between one, two, and three. This system emerges in human infants at about five months of age.

Second, a system for discriminating large, approximate numerical magnitudes—the difference between a set of about 10 things and a set of about 20 things.

Third, a system of natural number concepts that children construct as they learn verbal counting. This takes place between about the ages of two and a half and four years.

Fourth and Fifth are systems first seen in children when they navigate: understanding the geometry of the surrounding layout and identifying landmark objects.

Spelke reviewed the literature on a large number of infants to see if there were any sex differences in the development of these five systems. Again the answer is no. There is, she notes, a biological foundation to mathematical and scientific reasoning that emerges in children before any formal instruction. These systems develop equally in males and females. "There's not a hint of an advantage for boys over girls in any of these five basic systems."

In fact, scientists are learning that infants' minds are much more complex than we thought. Alison Gopnik,[15] a Berkeley psychologist, writes that babies and very young children know, observe, explore, imagine, and learn more than we would ever have thought possible. In some ways, they are smarter than adults.

In 2007 in my lab at Berkeley, Tamar Kushnir and I discovered that preschoolers can use probabilities to learn how things work and that this lets them imagine new possibilities. We put a yellow block and a blue block on a machine repeatedly. The blocks were likely but not certain to make the machine light up. The yellow block made the machine light up two out of three times; the blue block made it light up only two out of six times.

Then we gave the children the blocks and asked them to light up the machine. These children, who couldn't yet add or subtract, were more likely to put the high-probability yellow block, rather than the blue one, on the machine.

We also did the same experiment, but instead of putting the high-probability block on the machine, we held it up over the machine and the machine lit up. Children had never seen a block act this way, and at the start of the experiment, they didn't think it could. But after seeing good evidence, they were able to imagine the peculiar possibility that blocks have remote powers. These astonishing capacities for statistical reasoning, experimental discovery and probabilistic logic allow babies to rapidly learn all about the particular objects and people surrounding them.

Here's another powerful example of how children grasp pre-scientific concepts. And, Gopnik told us, she looked for gender differences in her data, but *"we've never found any consistent sex differences"* (emphasis added).

Both boys and girls have the ability to understand complicated ideas early on. In 2007, Laura Schulz and Elizabeth Baraff Bonawitz,[16] at MIT, demonstrated that when young children play, they are also exploring cause and effect. They showed nursery school kids two different toys. One had two levers and a duck and a puppet that popped up. The researchers showed one group of children that when you pressed one lever the duck appeared and when you pressed the other, the puppet appeared. The second group observed that when you pressed both levers at once both objects popped up, but they never got a chance to see what the levers did separately. This ploy obscured the causal relation between the levers and the pop-up objects.

At that point, the adults gave the children the toys to play with. The children in the first group played with the toy much less than the children in the second group. When the children already knew how the toy worked, they were less interested in exploring it. But the children in the second group spontaneously played with the toy, and just by playing around, they figured out how it worked.

Natural Selection?

Are men destined to be math geniuses, while women must always labor in the trenches? Some argue today that the overrepresentation of males at the upper tail of the distribution of math aptitude scores explains why there are more men in leadership positions in science and math.

But how accurate is this widely accepted perception? This gender gap isn't universal. Janet Hyde[17] reports, "If you look at high-end math performance, there is a preponderance of boys in some nations, but *no* gender gap or a preponderance of girls in others." More girls than boys scored in the top one percent in math performance in Iceland and Thailand, and there were equal numbers of girls and boys in the top one percent in Indonesia and the UK. The United States actually had one of the most lopsided ratios of boys to girls in the top one percent. Only Greece, Turkey, and Macao had more lopsided ratios. Without this cross-cultural perspective, we would think that all countries are like ours. They aren't. Most journalists just pick up the U.S. stats and of course buy the argument that what's true here is true everywhere, and then it's just a short step to accepting universal male superiority.

In fact, it used to be true that when it came to performance on highly complex math problems, boys did measurably better than girls. But no more. Today, girls are dramatically closing the gap at all levels of math ability. In fact, high math scores may have more to do with a nation's gender equality than with some mystical, innate male superiority. At the highest level of mathematical ability, the 99th percentile, the gender ratio favoring boys was linked to indicators of a country's gender equity. The higher the gender equity of a country, the more closely related were the girls' and boys' scores at this highest-of-the-high level of performance.[18]

With all this new information available, you'd think that parents and teachers would be strongly urging girls to take up careers in math and science. Not so. Janet Hyde[19] says, "The stereotype that boys do better at math is still held widely by teachers and parents, and teachers and parents guide girls, giving them advice about what courses to take, what careers to pursue. I still hear anecdotes about guidance counselors steering girls away from engineering, telling them they won't be able to do the math."

But do high SAT scores predict careers in math and science? In fact, no, according to an exhaustive 2006 review of major studies, funded by the National Academy of Sciences.[20] The study authors found no relationship between scoring in the upper tail of ability and eventual success in math/science careers. Of the college-educated professional workforce in mathematics, science, and engineering, fewer than one-third of the men had math SAT scores above 650, the lower end of the threshold typically presumed to be required for success in these fields. Clearly, not all these guys were Einsteins.

What, in fact, does create a successful science career? In 2007,[21] a group of children who scored in the upper one percent in mathematical reasoning ability at age 13 were assessed again when they were 33 years of age. What did the researchers learn?

Those who pursued careers in science and mathematics took more related coursework in high school, rated math and science courses as their favorites, and were interested in math and science. More of the highly gifted males than the females had these patterns of experiences and attitudes that were predictive of career choices in science and mathematics. (When these variables were accounted for, only one percent of the difference in careers was attributed to sex.)

High-ability males were found in one study to have unrealistically high self-competency beliefs; no such effect was found for females. In other words, boys think they're better than they actually are in math and science, which may boost their self-confidence. If you're a boy, you start to think early on that you're good at math, and if that belief prompts your parents to buy you math- and science-oriented toys, and you choose the toughest math courses, each of these small choices becomes a major force in your career development. The girl who sat next to you in second grade may have had more natural ability than you, but if she's not encouraged by her parents and teachers, her choices may be very different, and a top-level math career may never happen for her.

## The Truth About the Tests

We often hear that girls just don't score well overall on math exams, especially the SAT. That's not so.

- In 2009, using data from the United States, as well as international data, Janet Hyde and Janet Mertz,[22] both of the University of Wisconsin, found that U.S. girls now perform as well as boys on standardized math tests at all grade levels
- In 2008, a remarkable study was funded by the National Science Foundation[23] and published in *Science*, arguably the country's most prestigious research publication. This study was based on math scores from 7 million students in 10 states, tested in accordance with the federal No Child Left Behind Act. Moreover, these children were predominantly in public coed schools.

Researchers found, in every category, that girls did as well as boys. Even at the higher grades, when children were taking harder courses, there were absolutely no meaningful differences in the math scores of boys and girls. The strong takeaway message is that gender is simply not a predictor of math ability. So much for the Larry Summers argument.

It's important to note that even during the middle-school years—when girls' interest in math supposedly suffers a deep decline—there are no differences between boys' and girls' math test results. Middle school is not taking a huge toll on girls' academic performance, especially in math.

When new findings of a study that has been called "the nation's report card on math and science abilities"[24] were released in February 2007, the mainstream media virtually ignored the fact that 12th-grade girls were doing as well as 12th-grade boys across the board in math. Astonishingly, not one of the 37 newspaper articles found in a LexisNexis search on the study mentioned the fact that girls were on a par with boys on a range of math abilities, including algebra, geometry, measurement properties, data analysis, and other areas. On average, there was only a two-point difference between boys' and girls' overall math scores on a test in which scores ranged from 0 to 500, according to the National Assessment of Educational Progress.

As for the SAT exams, they are designed to predict math grades for college freshmen—and they don't even do that very well. There has been much debate about gender bias in the tests, and efforts are under way to correct it, but these efforts are still a work in progress. If the tests were valid, then women should do less well than men in their first-year math courses. The reality is different. Women do as well as men in their first-year mathematics courses, even though their average math SAT scores are not as high. How boys or girls do in math depends on the content of the test and on the way it is structured. Diane Halpern,[25] of Claremont McKenna College, notes that the usual male advantage on the math GRE (the test most students take to get into graduate school) can go up or down depending on how the problems are presented and what skills are required to solve them.

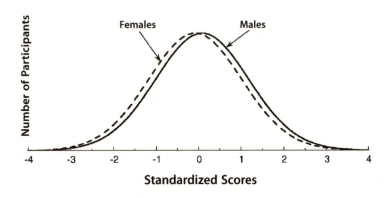

FIGURE 4.1    Gender Differences in Mathematics Performance
*Source:* J. S. Hyde, "Gender Differences in Mathematics Performance:
A Meta-Analysis," *Psychological Bulletin* 107 (1990): 149.

Overall, Halpern says, while boys score higher on tests of mathematics, girls achieve higher grades in math classes. One Pennsylvania high school senior, a member of the National Honor Society and in the top 10 percent of her class, scored lower on her SAT test than did many of the boys in her class who had much lower academic rank. But she went on to graduate magna cum laude from the University of Pittsburgh.[26] The test, she said, "didn't really predict how I did, that's for sure." Some people believe that the SAT resembles a fast-paced game, like a computer game, that puts a premium on strategic guesswork. Boys tend to perform better in that kind of situation. But when girls get coaching on how to take the test, their scores improve.

For the real story on boys, girls, and math, look at figure 4.1.

Psychologist Janet Hyde[27] of the University of Wisconsin, in a meta-analysis  of the math scores of 4 million students, found few differences. Boys outperformed girls in 51 percent of the studies, girls outperformed boys in 43 percent, and there was no gender difference in 5 percent of the studies. Sex differences were tiny.

Diane Halpern,[29] in a definitive overview of math and cognitive abilities that are supposed to show substantial sex differences, found such differences to be trivial. Overall, she says, while there are slight differences, boys and girls are far more alike than different.

Raging Hormones?

Some researchers argue that the male hormones that kick in at puberty give boys a big edge in math. Michael Gurian, for example, says that high testosterone enables boys to perform better on math tests than girls. In their book *Brain Sex*,[30] Anne Moir and David Jessel make the same claim, as does Steven Rhoads[31] in *Taking Sex Differences Seriously*. In *The Female Brain*,[32] Luann Brizendine writes: "When boys and girls enter their teens, their math and science abilities are equal. But as estrogen floods the female brain, females start to focus intensely on emotions and communication, girls start to lose interest in pursuits that require more solitary work and prefer interaction with others." This, she explains, is why girls don't do well in math.

If these statements were true, we'd see boys' scores at this age soaring ahead of girls' scores. If girls' brains aren't hardwired to do math, then their scores should start lower than those of males and stay that way. But in 2001 sociologists Erin Leahey and Guang Guo,[33] at the University of North Carolina, Chapel Hill, looked at some 20,000 math scores of kids age 4 to 18 and found no differences of any magnitude, even in areas that are supposedly male domains, such as reasoning skills and geometry. In the graph (fig. 4.2), notice that the trajectories of male and female math scores are nearly identical.

This finding astonished the researchers, who said, "Based on prior literature . . . we expected large gender difference to emerge

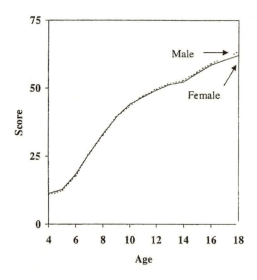

FIGURE 4.2    Math Trajectories from Ages 4 to 18
*Source*: E. Leahey and G. Guo, "Gender Differences in Mathematical Trajectories,"
*Social Forces* 80: 713–732.

as early as junior high school, but our results do not confirm this."
The only male advantage, which shows up in late high school, is a
meager 1.5 percent.

If male hormones ignited boys' math abilities like a Roman can-
dle, you'd expect to see a great difference in boys' and girls' scores in
the early teen years. Look at the graph. It doesn't happen.

Arguments over the effect of hormones on math performance
remain lively in academia, but obviously hormones don't act in
a vacuum. Whatever their effect, they act in concert with many
other factors—environment, culture, personality, social expectations, stereotypes—making it hard to pinpoint exactly what
changes hormones are responsible for. But they don't play the
major role in math ability—if they did, the graph would look
much different.

## A-hunting We Will Go

In *Brain Sex*, Moir and Jessel state that male superiority in spatial abilities is not in dispute—men can "picture things, their shape, position, geography, and proportion." Deborah Blum, a Pulitzer Prize-winning journalist, proclaims in her book *Sex on the Brain*[34] the "well-documented superiority of boys in spatial analysis at handling maps and numbers"—and cites this superiority to bolster her conclusion that male and female brains evolved differently because of different roles in prehistory. As one reviewer put it, "Basically, men had to keep maps in their heads because they were wandering all over the forest cruising for chicks. Women, meanwhile, were staying home tending the nest."

The voices of some other researchers join in unequivocal unison: "Males have decidedly better spatial skill than females" (L. J. Harris, *Sex Differences in Spatial Ability*).[35] "Boys excel in visual-spatial ability. Male superiority on visual-spatial tasks is fairly consistently found in adolescence and adulthood, but not in childhood" (E. E. Maccoby and C. N. Jacklin, *Psychology of Sex Differences*).[36] "Sex differences favoring males have been found quite consistently [in the area of spatial abilities] so perhaps there is a grain of truth to the old stereotype that women tend to have severe difficulties deciphering maps!" (H. Lips, A. Myers, and N. Colwill, *Sex Differences in Ability*).[37]

If these generalizations prove to hold water, what do they mean? If women can't read maps, have trouble with directions, can't visualize objects in space, can't create computer models of objects that don't yet exist, then they will be unfit for a whole range of occupations. They can't be commercial pilots, they shouldn't drive trucks or taxis, they shouldn't be engineers, they can't design systems, they can't follow blueprints, they can't navigate at sea, and they can't command spaceships.

In *Why Men Don't Listen and Women Can't Read Maps*, an international best seller, Barbara and Allan Pease[38] declare that because women didn't hunt big game, they can't read maps, can't parallel-park, and can't play video games. Occupational titles that women should not attempt to acquire, they say, since "their brain bias is not suited to these areas," include engineer, air traffic controller, architect, flight deck officer, actuary, and accountant.

With this media narrative all around us, it's oh-so-easy to project our 1950s, TV-enhanced fantasies of Dad at work and Mom in front of the stove at home back into the depths of time. We can imagine our hunter-gatherer ancestors with the women and children huddled by the campfire at their "home bases" waiting patiently for the hunter males to return.

But anthropologist Richard Potts,[39] director of the Human Origins Program of the Smithsonian National Museum of Natural History, throws a monkey wrench in that lovely domestic scene.

Potts examined the assemblages of bones, tools, and rocks on which the "home base" theories were built and argued that early humans did not dwell in one place for long periods of time, for the simple reason that the remains of large carnivores were found along with human remains. Humans would not have hung around in the presence of these carnivores. Rather, Potts sees the sites as places where early humans stopped for a time, and stored caches of tools and weapons.

In prehistory, men, women, and children were constantly on the move, all involved in the endless hunt for food, in which all took part. Often, men drove large game toward nets where women and children were waiting to ensnare them.

Primatologist Linda Fedigan,[40] of the University of Alberta, thinks that Potts's work should overturn old "Flintstone" images of prehistory. "We can perhaps finally free our minds of the image of dawn-age women and children waiting at campsites for the return of the provisioners."

In fact, women were as active in foraging as men, which is how humans got their food through much of prehistory. Success in foraging requires many of the same spatial abilities required by hunting: reading animal signs, making mental maps, remembering directions.

It makes evolutionary sense to imagine that successful females as well as males were those who had good spatial abilities.

And recently, anthropologists have found much evidence of female hunting. In the Ice Age, women used nets to capture hares, whose remains are plentiful in sites from the Upper Paleolithic era. Inuit women and others carried bows and arrows, especially blunt arrows designed for hunting birds. Wouldn't taking aim at a bird in flight and hitting it with an arrow or hunting agile Ice Age hares with a net have sharpened women's skills at dealing with distance and space? Wouldn't the sex that spent centuries doing these things have developed a brain that would make it possible to park a Chrysler? Such women must have had highly developed spatial abilities, as do the 42,000 female pilots in the United States, the women who command or fly on the space shuttle, serve in the armed services as Apache helicopter pilots and fighter pilots taking off from aircraft carriers, become military police commanders, tactical intelligence analysts, and combat engineers. So why do we believe the myth that only men have superior spatial abilities?

For one thing, only recently have women been permitted to hold jobs that require such skills. If you grow up seeing only male engineers, pilots, and truck drivers, then of course you accept the "fact" that only men have the ability to do such jobs. Also, many women grew up seeing only boys throwing baseballs, playing with erector sets, and building model airplanes. And even today we read in our college textbooks that "play patterns [of boys] reflect an evolved adaptation that prepares them for hunting and primitive warfare. Both the predisposition of this type of behavior and the play behavior itself may shape the male brain in ways that allow them to perform better than females on spatial tasks."

It's not surprising, then, that we hear such confident assertions about men's superior spatial abilities. But are they true?

One meta-analysis of cognitive differences[41] found a consistent male superiority, but a tiny one: Gender accounted for no more than 1 to 5 percent of the variance in cognitive abilities. With these numbers, knowing the sex of a child would tell you virtually nothing about his or her cognitive ability. (Spatial ability is one form of cognitive ability.) Another meta-analysis[42] of 100 studies found the magnitude of the sex-related cognitive differences to be "trivial"; others indicate no special male advantage, save perhaps a small one in mentally rotating an object in three dimensions (1 to 5 percent). Others claim that there are "pockets" of abilities where one sex or the other tends to excel. According to Diane Halpern, females are somewhat better at rapid access to and retrieval of information stored in memory, and males are somewhat better at the ability to maintain and manipulate mental representations. But the best available research shows us that the difference between males and females in spatial abilities is small indeed.

## Round and Round

One area where boys consistently outperform girls is "mental rotation"—the ability to imagine how objects will appear when they are rotated in two- or three-dimensional space. But before we look to Stone Age male hunters to find an explanation, consider a basic scientific principle: The most logical explanation for a phenomenon is probably the correct one. To account for boys' spatial abilities, we need look no further than their tendency to play more games in childhood such as football, baseball, and blocks than do girls. One study[43] found that boys threw better than girls did with their dominant arm—but when the kids were asked to throw with their other arm, there were no gender differences. If biology alone determined throwing ability, then boys would throw better than girls with either arm. The researchers concluded that practice, not a hardwired ability, turned boys into better throwers.

More evidence that mental rotation skills involve learned behavior comes from an intriguing new study by a Canadian team.[44] The scientists observed that young people who played video games that involved tracking (such as those in which the gamer virtually shoots and kills attacking "bad guys") had superior mental rotation skills. Instead of just noting that the males did better than the females, and chalking the difference up to female brains, or hormones or male hunting in prehistory, the team took another step. The low scorers were divided into two groups; one group spent ten hours playing tracking video games, while the others did not get such training. What happened? The training almost completely eradicated the gender gap in mental rotation skills. And when the researchers checked back six months later, the group that had received the training had retained the gains they made.

Clearly, one of the things we need to do is develop games that appeal to girls and that involve the same sort of tracking skills that the boy-oriented games provide. Such games don't have to be violent. We could imagine, for example, a game called "Save the Polar Bears," in which players have to track and snare the bears as they dash across the ice or plunge into the icy waters. The goal: to send the bears to protected habitats where they would not be drowned by melting Arctic ice.

In fact, recent meta-analyses[45] have shown that children and adults can improve their spatial skills with training. Importantly, research[46] finds that sex differences on the math SAT can be eliminated when the effect of mental-rotation ability is removed. One possible educational intervention for females and males would be to teach them multiple ways to solve problems using both verbal and spatial solution strategies, thereby allowing for more flexibility in overall problem solving.

Women can learn to enhance their spatial skills and thereby enjoy greater success in STEM (science, technology, engineering, and mathematics) fields. A course that has been taught for more than ten years at Michigan Technological University[47] is based on the idea that sketching three-dimensional objects is a significant factor (but not the only factor) in the development of these skills. The gains made by students on these spatial-skills tests as a result of participation in the course were statistically significant. Both men and women who initially scored low on spatial tests benefited from the instruction. And the gains they made were retained over their four years at college. The message here is that at all levels of education, for both boys and girls, we need curricula specifically targeted at learning spatial skills.

Parents can also be key to encouraging their children's math skills, of all types. A 10-year study of 4,000 children and 2,000 parents, conducted by Jacqueline Eccles,[48] of the University of Michigan, found that parents offer far more encouragement to boys than to girls to engage in problem-solving activities—playing with Legos, for instance—that may give them an early advantage in spatial skills. And parents are more likely to attribute a boy's success in this realm to "natural talent," whereas a girl is seen as "hardworking."

We will no doubt see the supposedly "natural" male advantage in all spatial skills fall away as girls play more high-level soccer, baseball, basketball, tennis, and golf at an early age. Does Annika Sorenstam's hand-eye coordination need buffing up? Does Michele Kwan seem to have problems with visualizing rotation in space as she does a perfect triple flip? Is Mia Hamm unable to traverse the shortest route to where the ball is going to be? Hardly. Serena and Venus Williams certainly have no trouble seeing objects in space. It can be argued that their father virtually manufactured his girls as tennis stars. After seeing how much women could make on the pro circuit, he gave his daughters rackets almost as soon as they could walk and mapped their careers from toddlerhood. They hit tens of thousands of tennis balls from a very early age and were grandly rewarded for doing well.

Math Aversion

In our culture, as the Harvard melee shows, a toxic feedback loop exists that puts shackles on girls' future earnings and accomplishment. More and more, research finds that individuals base their career choices on what they *believe* to be their abilities rather than what their abilities actually are. Over time, children construct their own self-perceptions, which are based on their parents' messages.

Children then integrate these messages into their own self-beliefs, and ultimately use them in choosing a college major or a career. And mothers in particular have a strong and long-lasting influence on those choices. For example:

One longitudinal study[49] looked at mothers' attitudes towards their sixth-grade children's math ability and interviewed the children again 12 years later. As it turned out, mothers' perceptions made little difference to boys, but were crucial for girls. When mothers were confident in their daughters' abilities, the girls were likely to choose careers in math. When mothers thought their girls would not succeed in math, the girls generally did not follow that path (fig. 4.3).

Even when parents take their kids on a "learning" trip, girls can get shortchanged. In one study[50] of kids' and parents' visits to a science museum (2004), the girls and boys were equally engrossed in the exhibits. But boys were three times more likely than girls to hear explanations from their parents about what they were seeing. This gender difference popped up with kids as young as 1 to 3 years of age. Parents may be involved, quite unconsciously, in creating a gender bias in science learning years before their kids ever even see the inside of a science classroom.

One 2000 study of third- and fourth-grade children and their parents and teachers found that parents and teachers said they believed that boys were more talented in math—even though the test scores of the actual children showed *no* gender difference in math.[51]

Girls too often are sabotaged early on. For example, teachers of sixth-grade math students believed that boys were more talented at math than girls, even when the actual kids in their classes scored equally on tests. Parents of sixth graders had less confidence in daughters than in sons—*regardless of their girls' actual abilities and performance*

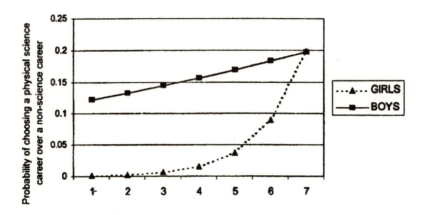

FIGURE 4.3    Relation Between Mothers' Perceptions (Sixth Grade) and
Young Adults' Career Choices (Ages 24 to 25)
*Source*: M. M. Bleeker and J. E. Jacoby, "Achievement in Math and Science: Do
Mothers' Beliefs Matter 12 Years Later?" *Journal of Educational Psychology* 96,
no. 1 (2004): 13.

*scores*. This attitude held true even when girls had higher grades in
math than boys. Teachers and parents, it seems, often ignore the
reality in front of their eyes and see, instead, the stereotypes. So do
the kids themselves.[52]

Even worse, it has been estimated that nearly half the girls interested in math careers have actually been discouraged from taking
advanced math courses. One high school guidance counselor told a
visiting math professor, "I'll be honest with you. I don't encourage
girls to go into mathematics. They wouldn't be good at it, and in any
case, what would they do with it?"[53]
There is a veritable mountain of evidence showing that girls veer
away from math and science at a very early age: Children learn that
boys are supposed to be better at math than girls, and the down-
ward spiral begins.

In the third and fourth grades, boys and girls like math equally. There's no change in fifth and sixth grade for boys, but girls' preference declines. Between fourth and twelfth grades, the percentage of girls who say they like science decreases from 66 to 48 percent.[54]

In those same years, the percentage of girls who say they would prefer not to study math any more goes from 9 percent to a whopping 50 percent.[55]

As grade levels increase, both girls and boys increase their perceptions of math as useful for men. By eighth grade, girls are less likely than boys to enjoy science or math and seem to have less confidence in these subjects.[56]

A 2004 study of college-age women seniors majoring in math-related careers found that women who bought into the idea that women were less able than men were likely to want to change their majors and had less interest in graduate school.[57]

In the light of all these data, it's hard to believe its coincidence or "choice" that makes girls' enjoyment of math and science dip so severely. It's not that girls just don't "like" math and science, as some pundits insist. Rather, the culture has convinced them that they don't belong in these fields. And many girls do buy these ideas—both consciously and unconsciously. The more they accept such ideas, the less likely they are to seriously pursue math careers. Girls get the message that math is not for them, even when they are performing as well as boys. This phenomenon is called "the leaky pipeline," in which talented girls are lost to math and science from preschool on.

The power of stereotypes has been dramatically documented by the work of psychologists Claude Steele[58] and Joshua Aaronson on "stereotype threat." Certain groups—such as African Americans and women—can suffer an extra burden of anxiety because they are aware of the negative stereotype of the group to which they belong. When they are told that women aren't good at math, women do much worse on a test than when they are told nothing at all before the test. Without the negative information, they score nearly as well as men. Figure 4.4 shows the dramatic power of stereotypes.

Stereotype threat also hobbles girls in the vital areas of visual-spatial abilities, which are are key to success in such fields as engineering, chemistry, medicine, and architecture. These are areas that will offer high-paying, prestigious jobs in the years ahead. In a 2009 study,[59] the researchers found that women scored highest on tests measuring these abilities when they were led to believe that there were no gender differences on the study tasks. Strikingly, when they were told that men do better on theses tasks—or when they were given no information, allowing cultural stereotypes to operate, they did poorly.

If teachers make it clear that there are no gender differences in boys' and girls' abilities relating to STEM fields, then they can reduce the impact of stereotype threat and level the educational playing field for the children in their classes.

Despite all this research, beliefs about girls' innate inability in math persist even when the facts say the contrary. And, unfortunately, discrimination against women is alive and well. Why, indeed, do females fail to make headway in academia in math and science? One answer comes from a study in which two résumés were sent to college professors to evaluate—sometimes with a male name attached, sometimes a female name. One résumé was a "walk on water" scholar who had the best of everything. The other was an accomplished but not spectacular scientist, like the résumés that usually come in to academic search committees. Everyone said they'd hire the "walk on water" candidate, male or female. That was a no-brainer. But when it came to the good but not spectacular candidate, it was a very different story.

Harvard's Elizabeth Spelke[60] notes, "The male was rated as having higher research productivity." The scientists "looked at the same number of publications and thought, 'good productivity' when the name was male, and 'less good productivity' when the name was female.

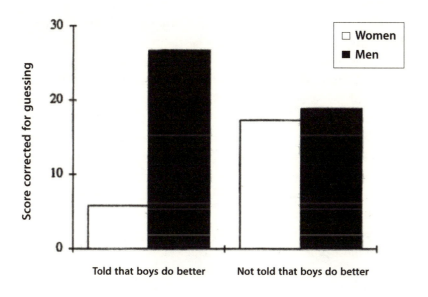

FIGURE 4.4   Mean Performance on a Difficult Math Test as a Function of
Gender and Test Characterization
*Source*: Adapted from C. M. Steele, "A Threat in the Air: How Stereotypes Shape the
Intellectual Identities and Performance of Women and African Americans," *American
Psychologist* 52 (1997): 613–629.

Same thing for teaching experience. The very same list of courses was
seen as good teaching experience when the name was male, and less
good teaching experience when the name was female. In answer to
the question would they hire the candidate, 70 percent said yes for the
male, 45 percent for the female. If the decision were made by majority
rule, the male would get hired and the female would not."

The professors were asked to express reservations about the
good candidates, and tellingly, "those kinds of reservations were
expressed *four times more often* when the name was female than
when the name was male." And this wasn't just a "guy" thing. Both
men and women expressed reservations in a sexist fashion—attesting

to the way stereotypes get lodged in our heads even when we don't know they are there.

This bias was underlined in a graphic way in a country that is one of the most egalitarian in the world—Sweden. The peer-review system of the Swedish Medical Research Council (MRC),[61] one of the main funding agencies for biomedical research, does not evaluate women and men on an equal basis for its prestigious fellowships. When men and women were rated for scientific competence, males fared far better—even when they weren't as good as women.

Researchers found that a female applicant had to be 2.5 times more productive than the average male applicant to receive the same competence score as the male received.

The most productive group of female applicants (those with 100 points or more for publication, research, etc.) was the only group of women judged to be as competent as men. Even then, astonishingly, these female achievers were judged only as competent as the *least* productive group of male applicants (who had fewer than 20 points).

This study provides direct evidence that the peer-review system is subject to sex bias.

Teachers Play a Part

Are the female teachers of little girls unwittingly infecting their students with math anxiety as early as first grade? Do we need to intervene earlier than we thought to make sure that girls are not irretrievably lost to such high-paying jobs as engineer, mathematician, computer scientist, physicist, and chemist?

That's the troubling message of a new, first-of-its-kind study (2010).[62] Sian L. Beilock, an associate professor of psychology at the University of Chicago (and her colleagues), found that female elementary school teachers who lack confidence in their own math skills seem to be passing their anxiety along to the first- and second-grade girls they teach. The research team studied 52 boys and 65 girls who were in classes taught by 17 different teachers. Ninety percent of U.S. elementary school teachers are women, as were all of those in this study. The study was published in *Proceedings of the National Academy of Sciences*.

This is the gloomy story, and, indeed, the media cast it as just another piece of bad news that would make parents of girls chew more antacid tablets. For example, *USA Today* headlined "Girls May Learn Math Anxiety from Female Teachers." And *Discover* warned, "Female Teachers' Math Anxiety May Give Girls the Arithmetic Jitters." But there may be a silver lining in this story for parents. Even if your daughter has a teacher with high math anxiety, it's not inevitable that she's going to have problems with math. When you dig deeper into the study, you find that the researchers examined the mechanism connecting teachers' anxiety to their students' math achievement. It turns out that parents (or others) can "vaccinate" girls against their teachers' math anxiety.

Teachers' anxiety alone didn't do the damage. If girls already had a belief that "girls aren't good at math," then their achievement suffered.

But the girls who didn't buy into that stereotype, who thought that of course they could be good at math, didn't tumble into an achievement gulf. The girls who internalized the stereotype *and* had anxious teachers got a double whammy.

This problem was not seen at the beginning of the school year, but became clear by the end of the year, after the children had had considerable contact with their teacher. The researchers say, "Indeed, by the end of the school year, girls who endorsed this stereotype had significantly worse math achievement than girls who did not and than boys overall. In early elementary school, where the teachers are almost all female, teachers' math anxiety carries consequences for girls' math achievement by influencing girls' beliefs about who is good at math."

But, too often, not only do girls buy into the "boys are the ones good at math" belief, but their parents do as well. One teacher we interviewed, Carolynn Klein, of the Duke School in North Carolina, remembers that the mother of a first grader said that her daughter was not good at mathematics. (She couldn't balance her checkbook or change a $100 bill?)

However, pointing a finger at parents doesn't let teachers off the hook. A German study in 2005 found that third- and fourth-grade teachers believed that boys were better in math, in spite of the fact that girls consistently had grades equal to those of boys. The girls bought into their teachers' beliefs, even when they were at odds with the girls' own test scores.

It is especially troubling that in the United States, elementary education majors at the college level have the highest math anxiety of any major. In the classroom, they can be part of the mechanism that passes along a virus of underachievement to girls. It's not a message that teachers want to hear, but they owe it to their students to really look at their own beliefs.

And teachers can do it, if they try. Carolynn says, "I never thought of myself as a math person." In fact, she said to herself, "Okay, that's why I teach kindergarten." But it soon became clear to her that kids need to master math and science early on, but can't if their teachers aren't up to speed. Now, thanks to lots of training and experience, she says, "I have gotten so much more skilled as a mathematician."

## The Good News

When Larry Summers made his explosive comments, he was talking mainly about the dearth of female professors in science and engineering at elite universities. From atop the pile at Harvard, the picture could indeed have seemed grim. It's what he didn't see that makes the difference. Could the structure of universities themselves be the problem? The answer is a resounding "yes!" If you look only at universities as an indication of who is talented in math and science, you will get a skewed picture. Women do spectacularly better, a 2004 study shows, in non-hierarchical workplaces.[63]

Female scientists working in biotech firms have a much higher probability of being in a position to lead research teams than do their female colleagues in academia. In universities, women were 60 percent less likely to be supervising than men. In biotech, women were 7.9 times more likely to be in supervisory jobs than in universities. (There were no differences for men between academia and biotech.)

MIT was a good example of the bias against women. A 1999 report[64] found that through subtle and largely unconscious discrimination, most of the senior female scientists in the school had received lower salaries and fewer resources for research than their male counterparts, and had been excluded from significant roles within their departments.

Conservative critics still argue today that the women probably weren't as good as the men, accounting for their lack of success. But in a 2006 report on the same study, evidence was presented that debunks that idea. The women were actually *more* accomplished than the men. For example, they were far more likely to have been named to the National Academy of Sciences, to be members of the American Academy of Arts and Sciences, and to have been awarded the National Medal of Science. Dean Robert J. Birgeneau took prompt action to redress inequities. Today, MIT's Nancy Hopkins reports, women scientists at the university are thriving.

Female scientists are shattering the glass ceiling. In 2009 four Nobel laureates in the sciences were women, a new record:

Elinor Ostrom, 76, who made history by being the first woman to win the Nobel Memorial Prize in Economic Sciences

Elizabeth H. Blackburn, 60, and Carol W. Greider, 48, who shared the 2009 Nobel Prize in physiology or medicine with Jack W. Szostak for their work in solving the mystery of how chromosomes protect themselves from degrading when cells divide

Ada Yonath, 70, of Israel, who shared the Nobel Prize in chemistry for atom-by-atom description of ribosomes

If we want our daughters to thrive in math and science, we have to peel away the layers of myth and misinformation about women's lack of ability in these areas due to their hormones or their brains. With predictions that careers in the areas of science, technology, engineering, and mathematics (STEM) will dominate the workforce of the twenty-first century, girls will suffer if they don't get early encouragement in these areas the way boys do.

*MIT News* reports[65] that American teens are embracing STEM subjects with increasingly positive attitudes; yet "many lack the necessary encouragement from mentors and role models in these fields." Donna Milgram, the executive director of the National Institute for Women in Trades, Technology, and Science[66] (IWITTS) emphasizes the fact that girls' performance has little to do with actual skills and a lot to do with perceptions and confidence. "For females, confidence is a predictor of success in the STEM classroom. They are much less likely to retain interest if they feel they are incapable of mastering the material. Unfortunately, two factors work against female confidence level: 1) most girls will actually have less experience with STEM course content than their male counterparts and 2) males tend to overplay their accomplishments while females minimize their own." A study of Carnegie Mellon Computer Science Ph.D. students[67] found that even when male and female students were doing equally well in terms of grades, female students reported feeling less comfortable. Fifty-three percent of males rated themselves as "highly prepared" in contrast to *zero* percent of females.

Girls often don't believe in their own problem-solving ability, and they can be tentative instead of bold when it comes to jumping in to tackle a problem before them. "Teachers," says Milgram, "can address this by such activities as: 1) having them take apart old equipment and put it together again, 2) creating 'scavenger hunt' exercises that force them to navigate through [computer] menus and 3) emphasizing that they are learning the problem solving process and that this is equally important to learning the content of the lesson and insisting that they figure out hands-on exercises on their own."

When girls realize that they can learn to problem-solve as well as boys, they lose their tentativeness and rise to the challenge. As Lise Eliot reminds us, "Math and science have been the source of much of humanity's greatest creativity. We are not doing enough to harness this creative talent in American children in general, and girls in particular."

But we can change. Maybe the next Einstein will be a girl whose parents and teachers never told her she couldn't do math.

# 5 WORD PLAY

A peculiar concern about boys and books has long been a hallmark of American society. Sometimes we worry that boys are reading too much; sometimes that they are not reading enough—and reading badly to boot.

In the early 1900s, urgent polemics appeared in newspapers, books, and magazines, warning that young men were spending too much time in school with female teachers and that the constant interaction with women was robbing them of their manhood. They were becoming too "bookish." In Congress, Senator Albert Beveridge of Indiana railed against overeducation. He urged young men to "avoid books and in fact avoid all artificial learning, for the forefathers put America on the right path by learning completely from natural experience."[1]

What boys needed, the experts said, was time outdoors, rubbing elbows with one another and learning from male role models, not books. That's what led—at least in part—to the founding of the Boy Scouts in 1910.

Now the cry has been raised again. This time the narrative is not that boys do too much reading, but that they don't do enough. The new message is that boys are lagging far behind girls, and may be so inherently hobbled verbally that they need massive help. The media hyped America's new "boy crisis" in magazine cover stories, a PBS documentary, and countless newspaper articles.

Boys, these reports lament, are displaying poorer verbal skills and need special "boy books" to help them. Boys are at a disadvantage in the many classrooms headed by female teachers, who are supposedly hostile to the male sex. One high school student in Massachusetts even filed a federal lawsuit claiming that his school is biased against males.[2]

Houston neurologist Bruce Perry, quoted in *Newsweek*,[3] claimed that because of boys' hardwired disadvantages, putting girls and boys in the same classes is a "biologically disrespectful model of education." And the *New Republic*[4] claimed that a "verbally drenched curriculum" is "leaving boys in the dust."

But are American boys actually in reading free fall? Are they verbal basket cases?

Not really.

The alarming statistics on which the notion of a boy crisis is based are rarely broken out by race or class. When the data are analyzed separately by race and class, the whole picture changes. It becomes clear that if there is a crisis, it's among inner-city and rural boys. White suburban boys, on average, are not dropping out of school, avoiding college, or lacking in verbal skills.[5] But the overall picture for poor minority boys and girls is truly alarming.

When it comes to differences in academic achievement, race and class completely swamp gender. The Urban Institute[6] reports that 76 percent of students who live in middle- to higher-income areas are likely to graduate from high school, while only 56 percent of students who live in lower-income areas are likely to do so. Among whites in the Boston public schools in 2003–2004, for every 100 males who graduated, 104 females did.[7] A tiny gap. But among blacks, for every 100 males who graduated, 139 females did.

Florida's graduation rates[8] among all students showed a striking picture of race and class: in 2003, 80 percent for Asians, 61 percent for whites, 48 percent for Hispanics, and 47 percent for blacks. This situation urgently needs attention.

But this reality is not what's being marketed by the media. The idea being hyped is that *all* boys are in trouble, that this is a new phenomenon, and that all boys must have their own dumbed-down "boy" books that lack nuance or emotion.

*National Review*: Without action-packed narratives, boys will be bored, disaffected, and disruptive.[9]

*Atlanta Journal-Constitution*: Even when boys are reading a book, you will see tapping of their feet or their eyes darting about in exploration.[10]

*Hartford Courant*: Because boys don't want to read books from beginning to end, informational texts are ideal.[11]

*New York Times* columnist David Brooks: Boys ought to be given books about combat, to hold their interest.[12]

But the real story is very different. The most recent—and probably the most reliable—word on the issue comes from a report using data compiled by the National Assessment of Educational Progress, a federally funded accounting of student achievement that has been gathering data since 1971. In June 2006, the Washington-based think tank Education Sector reported that over the past three decades boys' test scores are mostly up, more boys are going to college, and more are getting bachelor's degrees.[13]

The report labeled the "boy crisis" as greatly overstated. "But the truth is far different from what these accounts suggest," the report states. "The real story is not bad news about boys doing worse; it's good news about girls doing better." Focusing on gender differences, the report cautions could sidetrack efforts to put more education dollars into inner-city and rural schools, where both boys and girls desperately need better academic resources.

According to Education Sector, reading achievement by 9-year-old boys increased 15 points on a 500-point scale between 1971 and 2004, and 9-year-old girls' scores during that period increased 7 points, remaining 5 points ahead of boys. Reading achievement for 13-year-olds improved 4 points for boys and 3 points for girls, with girls 10 points ahead. Among 17-year-olds, there was almost no change in reading achievement, with girls up 1 point, boys down 1 point and girls 14 points ahead.

These very reliable data hardly paint a picture of boys sinking faster than the *Titanic* in verbal abilities.

Still, some people ask whether feminist teachers are declaring war on boys, favoring girls while putting down boys, making them read books about "girl" stuff, and telling them to sit still and shut up.

Nonverbal Boys?

Out of this crucible of alarm, a peculiar image of the "typical" boy has emerged in many media reports: he's unable to focus, can't sit still, hates to read, acts up in class, loves sports and video games, and gets in trouble a lot. Indeed, such boys do exist—it has long been established that boys suffer more from attention deficit disorder than girls do—and they need all the help they can get. But research shows that this picture does not reflect the typical boy. Boys, in fact, are as different from one another as they are from girls.

Nonetheless, some are advocating boys-only classrooms in which boys would be taught in boot-camp fashion, with less emphasis on verbal skills than coed classes would have.

But is there really strong evidence that most boys *inherently* lack verbal skills?

In a word, no. In 1988 University of Wisconsin psychologist Janet Hyde[14] synthesized data from 165 studies on verbal ability and gender. The results revealed a female superiority so slight as to be meaningless. You can see how alike boys and girls are in figure 5.1.

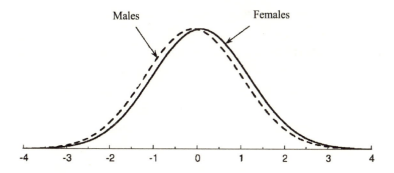

FIGURE 5.1    Gender Differences in Verbal Ability

And psychologist Diane Halpern,[15] of Claremont McKenna College, looked at many studies of verbal and math abilities and found that, overall, the gender differences were remarkably small.

When non-poor boys do fall behind in reading, what might the reasons be? Not hostile female teachers or hardwired inferiority. Many of us remember a time when boys had to read Shakespeare, Hardy, Longfellow, and other classics as early as eighth grade, when boys constituted the majority of valedictorians, dominated the debate teams, and edited the school newspapers. And then, as now, most boys were taught by female teachers. What has changed? Have boys' brains or hormones changed over the past thirty years? Not likely. But many boys do read less and play video games and watch TV more. Maybe one thing that's changed is our expectations. If we don't believe that boys have good verbal skills, they won't believe it either.

The Massachusetts student who brought the discrimination suit against his high school wants boys to be given credit for sports and to be excused from the school's community service requirement. But might that send the message to boys that they are inherently too dumb to get academic credit and too insensitive to be concerned about community issues?

Many, perhaps most, boys would be bored to tears in the kind of classroom that is now being described as "boy-friendly"—a classroom that would de-emphasize reading and verbal skills and would rely on rote learning and discipline—because it is really a remedial program in disguise. Such programs may indeed be needed for boys who have real problems in learning, but most boys don't have such problems. One group of studies found that although poor and working-class boys lag behind girls in reading when they get to middle school, boys in the wealthiest schools do not fall behind, either in middle school or in high school.[16] University of Michigan education professor Valerie Lee[17] looked at gender differences in verbal ability in this age group and found them "small to moderate."

However, a subtext of the boy-crisis stories seems to be a fear of girls' success. The fact that girls are succeeding academically touches a wellspring of psychic fear in some people. A 2003 *Businessweek*[18] cover asking whether boys were becoming the "Second Sex" featured a huge, smiling girl looming over a tiny, puzzled-looking boy. In some quarters, there is a peculiar fear that girls' success equals boys' failure. This is one of the main themes of the popular book by Christina Hoff Sommers,[19] *The War Against Boys*. Lacking much data and relying on a few anecdotes, she manages to spin a jeremiad about evil feminist teachers harming boys.

But where is the evidence of women taking over the world beyond school? Females earn considerably less than males and are under-represented in high-level jobs. As Jacqueline King, a director at the American Council on Education, told the *Seattle Times*,[20] "Do I think it's doomsday for the male gender? No. I look around the world, and it seems to me that men are still in charge."

The Education Sector report charges that the whole idea of a boy crisis has been used by conservative authors who accuse "misguided feminists" of lavishing resources on female students at the expense of males and by some liberals who say schools are "forcing all children into a teacher-led pedagogical box that is particularly ill-suited to boys' interests and learning styles."

There is, says the report, a "free market for theories about why boys are underperforming girls in school, with parents, educators, media, and the public choosing to give credence to the explanations that are the best marketed and that most appeal to their pre-existing preferences."

This sort of marketing, especially by the media, was probably behind the popularity of the notion, mentioned earlier, that women are the verbal sex while men are the strong and silent sex. This idea plays into the whole theory that males are not naturally good or comfortable with words, while women excel.

One statistic cited as proof of women's greater verbal ability is that they use more words per day than men do. The claim is that a woman uses 20,000 words per day, while a man uses only 7,000. Despite the widespread reports that this claim is accurate, it is not.

"It's been a common belief, but it just didn't fit," says James Pennebaker, chairman of the psychology department at the University of Texas at Austin and coauthor of a seven-year study of men's and women's speech.[21] In fact, both men and women use approximately 16,000 words a day.

Trailing Even in the Womb?

Despite all the scientific evidence that males aren't hardwired for poor verbal skills, the idea just won't die. A new twist on this notion is that male disadvantage starts very, very early, even before birth. It is generally agreed that girls' vocabulary is larger than boys' at an early age, but that boys quickly catch up. It is not clear how large the initial difference is or what factors account for it. At one extreme, some argue that decisive differences are innate and begin in the prenatal environment. Other researchers argue that social factors are critical. Who's right?

One prominent psychologist, Simon Baron-Cohen,[22] whom we discussed in great detail earlier, argues that fetal testosterone (FT) is critical in the development of vocabulary in toddlers. Boys, he says, start out behind in the wordplay race.

Baron-Cohen gets major press for his theories, so he provides a good case study for how theories can be widely accepted even when the science behind them is questionable and the data do not support them.

Baron-Cohen's area of expertise is autism, but he has been an influential voice for early gender differences for non-autistic children. He claims that the level of FT in utero is a causal factor in the vocabulary size of infants who are 18 months and 24 months of age. Specifically, the larger vocabulary of young girls compared to young boys is attributable, according to Baron-Cohen, to the influence of fetal testosterone in "shaping the neural mechanisms underlying communicative development." In other words, the more fetal testosterone in utero, the lower the child's vocabulary.

He claims to have hard data to support his theory. But how exactly was his study done? Baron-Cohen's clinic examined pregnant women who were all at high risk of carrying Down syndrome infants. The clinic drew amniotic fluid to test for Down syndrome; the fluid was frozen and then later analyzed for FT as well as other biological markers. The mothers in the study all gave birth to healthy babies, none of whom, as it turned out, actually had Down syndrome. The sample consisted of 87 infants (40 girls and 47 boys).

How did Baron-Cohen determine the children's vocabulary? He asked the mothers (highly non-objective reporters) to indicate how many words out of 416 their child could say at 18 and 24 months of age. As Baron-Cohen predicted, the higher the FT levels, the lower the vocabulary size.

These results sound very impressive and convincing. But are they? Not when you look closely. The study is riddled with problems.

First, high-risk mothers may not be typical of mothers in general. We have no way of knowing how the mothers' at-risk status may have affected their interactions—verbal and nonverbal—with their infants. No comparison group of non-high-risk mothers was tested.

Moreover, the usual method of assessing children's vocabulary is for objective researchers to videotape or audiotape children's speech production and then have independent analysts score the recordings for various types of speech utterances or patterns. In the Baron-Cohen study no such independent observations or measurements were done. Given the inherent unreliability of self-report data, it is striking that no test for any kind of bias was conducted.

Most importantly, a linkage between FT levels and vocabulary size was found, but only when the data from the two sexes were combined: When the data were analyzed for the two sexes separately, there was no relationship between fetal testosterone and vocabulary size. In other words, high fetal testosterone predicted low vocabulary for all children, not just for boys. Baron-Cohen offered no explanation for this unexpected result. Moreover, Baron-Cohen failed to provide the data needed to determine just how big the effect of FT on vocabulary size was. Consequently, the results raise serious questions about the role of FT in young boys' vocabulary size. Nevertheless, Baron-Cohen continues to repeat his argument to professional and lay audiences both in Europe and here in America.

It's also striking to note what Baron-Cohen didn't look at. Amazingly, he did not inquire about the mothers' or fathers' actual verbal interactions with their infants, nor did he do any observations of the parents interacting with their children. He did not even ask how much time per day on average the mothers talked to their children, read to their children, played word games with them, or watched TV or DVDs with them. In short, he and his team did not collect any data on actual time spent between the toddlers and their mothers and, as we will see, such parent-child variables appear to have powerful effects on young children's vocabulary.

In spite of all the media attention, Baron-Cohen's widely cited study tells us little about the magnitude of or the reasons for sex differences in the size of young boys' and girls' vocabulary. In fact, even one researcher who advocates for the importance of fetal testosterone cautions us not to overemphasize its power. John Manning,[23] professor of psychology at the University of Central Lancashire, says prenatal sex hormones exert only "a modest predisposing influence on human development" and "merely bias, rather than determine" the different behaviors we see in our sons and daughters

## Missing from the Media

A great many researchers could only wish for the kind of coverage that Baron-Cohen gets. These minions do solid work, get very different results, and no one gets to hear about them. In fact, many carefully conducted and scientifically sound studies have been done on infant and toddler vocabulary; most draw very different conclusions from Baron-Cohen's.

For example, there is growing evidence that it's not fetal testosterone—or the lack of it—that is key to vocabulary. The real story is in the way parents speak to their children. This isn't as new or sexy a tale as the one about prenatal hormones, but it makes much more sense. The case for parents' behavior and its critical impact on their children's verbal ability is a very strong one, much more impressive than the argument about FT.

In a 2006 study,[24] mothers of preverbal infants who were 6, 9, and 14 months old were observed in a free-play situation with gender-neutral toys. The behavior of the boys and girls was identical. However, the mother's behavior toward her child depended on the child's sex. With their little girls, mothers engaged in more conversation and expected their daughters to be more responsive than their sons. For example, a mother might ask her daughter, "You're playing with the octopus. You like that, right?" Or, "Look at you playing with your beads. Are you going to slide the red bead next?"

Mothers were much less likely to engage in such verbal exchanges with their sons. More often, they gave sons directions, such as "Come here" or checked on where their son was by calling his name.

Might these mothers be acting on expectations that their sons are not as verbal as their daughters? And, since the human brain develops in response to external stimuli, were the boys getting short-changed? Are mothers (and others) inadvertently teaching their very young children about gender roles through verbal interaction? That does appear to be the case

In 2007 researchers[25] observed mother-child interactions during both free play and bath time when the children were 10, 13, 17, and 21 months of age. Mothers spoke more to girls than to boys at the two older ages, ages at which children's vocabulary growth is typically accelerating. Recall that these are roughly the same ages at which Baron-Cohen studied vocabulary size.

Not only did mothers talk more to girls, but girls received more "responsive" and "supportive" talk from their moms than boys did. Mothers took note of what their daughters were doing and spoke about their activities and where they were at the time. These forms of maternal speech have been associated with positive outcomes in children. Sons received substantially more intrusive directives, like "Pick up that block."

Importantly, the kind of talk the girls heard was predictive of greater linguistic competence, while "the reverse is true for boys."

The researchers cited above asked a critical question: Might these differences in mothers' verbal interactions account for at least some of the advantage girls show in vocabulary development? Other studies suggest that the answer is yes. For example, the vocabulary that parents use while talking to preschool-age children predicts the children's vocabularies in second and third grades.[26] Maternal verbal interactions are important predictors of young children's verbal competence. And, unwittingly, parents provide very different verbal environments for their young sons and daughters.

In one major meta-analysis, Campbell Leaper, a psychologist at the University of California, Santa Cruz, and his colleagues[27] asked two key questions: (1) Do mothers and fathers differ in their language style with their children? (2) Do mothers differ in their language style with daughters versus sons?

These two questions go well beyond Baron-Cohen's research in that they inquire about the extent to which mothers and fathers differ in their verbal exchanges with their children, and they ask whether a mother's verbal behavior differs depending on whether she has a son or a daughter.

The researchers looked at six distinct forms of verbal interaction: (1) amount of talking, (2) supportive speech, (3) negative speech, (4) directive speech, (5) giving information; and (6) asking questions or requesting information. Importantly, none of the studies relied on self-report data. In most cases, mothers and fathers were observed by researchers in laboratory or home settings.

Overall, mothers tend to talk more than fathers and to use more supportive—as well as more negative—speech with their children. Moreover, mothers talk more and use more supportive and emotional speech with daughters than with sons. Fathers more often gave orders or asked questions.

These robust findings offer a stronger and more persuasive explanation for girls' early vocabulary advantage than fetal testosterone levels. If mothers talk more to their daughters than to their sons, girls have a comparatively greater chance of hearing and imitating words, an advantage that could easily account for their higher early vocabulary scores.

Not surprisingly, the child's age had a major effect on the mother's language behavior. For example, mothers talked more to their toddlers than fathers did. This is important because the toddler years are both the period of greatest language learning[28] and the time when children's gender identity is being formed.[29] They are also the time when mothers are speaking most differently to daughters and sons. Mothers are, in fact, enacting their own gender stereotypes by providing their daughters with more verbal input during these early years.[30] The apparent outcome is that daughters receive more verbal interaction than do sons. This difference may, in turn, be a major reason that young girls score higher in verbal skills than young boys do[31] and are more talk-oriented in their relationships than boys are.

So, instead of creating elaborate theories (which don't hold up) of fetal testosterone, which parents have no way of affecting, it would be much more helpful for parents to understand the dynamics of how they talk to their children, which they can do something about and which we know affects children's vocabularies. Any parent concerned about his or her son's verbal abilities could make sure that the language used with boys is rich and peppered with emotion, and that sons don't primarily get curt, simple verbal orders or requests.

Another factor may be who a young child's playmates are. In one provocative study of two-year-old fraternal twins, Robert Plomin[32] and his colleagues in London found that verbal development was importantly shaped by one's "speaking partner." Girls tend to be more verbal at this age, and having a female twin sister makes them even more so. Less verbal boys who have a twin brother have the lowest scores of all the groups studied. Boy and girl twins do better. So, female playmates for boys at young ages can help their verbal abilities. If boys hang out only with other boys, they are less verbal.

Another issue that's just starting to be examined is video games. Seventy-one percent of kids 2 to 11 who have a TV in their house have access to a video game system. As we noted earlier, these games can improve spatial ability in both boys and girls. But there might be a downside, especially for boys. A 2010 study[33] found that 6- to 9-year-old boys who were given video games had significantly worse reading and writing scores at the end of a four-month period than boys without the games. Math skills weren't affected.

Why does this happen? It may be that kids who have these games at home choose to spend more time sharpening their gaming skills than engaging in other activities that involve reading and writing. The fabulous graphics, the whiz-bang action, and the chance to compete trump reading a children's classic or even an adventure book. Those who look only at the classroom to explain boys' verbal skills may be missing a key element.

So this is a really complicated issue, and one we're just beginning to understand. But it takes more thought and careful research than the simple "innate behavior" theories. It is of course tempting to think that chemical reactions beyond our control are what really control our destinies—that we are "hardwired" for some behavior or another. It all sounds so "scientific" and cut-and-dried and appears to be simple to understand.

But what happens if parents and teachers absorb this stuff and get the idea that boys just don't have what it takes when it comes to verbal skills? Will their expectations for boys be lowered? One teacher quoted by *Newsweek* said she was giving boys more videos to watch and less material to read. This could spell disaster. Indeed, if boys aren't reading enough, there are many ways for parents and teachers to encourage them. But if boys begin to doubt their own abilities in this area (just as little girls as early as fourth grade begin to see math as "something that boys do"), their futures could be dimmed. Will parents begin to steer their boys away from majoring in English or dreaming of careers as writers because that's "girls' turf"?

If parents and teachers believe that males are naturally nonverbal, if they start to nudge boys toward low-level "action" texts or direct their reading toward "informational texts" (yawn), then boys will really be in trouble. They will be deprived of the richness of challenging, well-written stories that will heighten their imagination and deepen their understanding.

Leonard Sax,[34] for example, suggests that literature teachers should not ask boys about characters' emotions but should focus only on what the characters actually do. But teachers *should* focus on characters' emotions in teaching literature to girls. He also says that a boy who likes to read, who does not enjoy contact sports, and who does not have a lot of close male friends has a problem, even if he thinks he is happy. He should be firmly disciplined, required to spend time with "normal males," and made to play sports.

If we take this advice, boys with the potential to be the next John Updike, Ernest Hemmingway, Arthur Miller, or Robert Frost will be "firmly disciplined" and turned into barely competent linebackers. Society will be very much the poorer if this happens to our sons. Many men have found inspiration, compassion, meaning for their lives, and sometimes solace in the face of the deepest misfortune in serious literature

Robert Kennedy, in the throes of a seemingly intractable depression after the assassination of his brother Jack, spent a week in 1964 closeted in a room reading a book his sister-in-law Jackie had given him. It was *The Greek Way*, by Edith Hamilton. The book changed his life, writes *New York Times* columnist David Brooks.[35] "He carried his beaten, underlined and annotated copy around with him for years, pulling it from his pocket, reading sections aloud to audiences in what [biographer Evan] Thomas calls 'a flat, unrhythmic voice with a mournful edge.'"

Brooks reports that Kennedy found in the Greeks a sensibility similar to his own—heroic and battle-scarred but also mystical. Kennedy underlined this passage in Hamilton's book: "Life for him was an adventure, perilous indeed, but men are not made for safe havens. The fullness of life is in the hazards of life."

Ironically, David Brooks was getting at a deeper truth in his column on Kennedy than in his throwaway line about giving boys books about combat. He observes, "The lesson, of course, is about the need to step outside your own immediate experience into the past, to learn about the problems that never change, and bring back some of that inheritance. The leaders who founded the country were steeped in the classics, Kennedy found them in crisis, and today's students are lucky if they stumble on them by happenstance."

# 6 TOY CHOICE

We're often informed that boys "naturally" rush to play with guns and trucks, while girls just as naturally head for the dolls and tea sets. This, we're told, is biology at work, some "hardwired" impulse that has nothing to do with children's environment.

Is this so? Are we dealing with a reality dictated by nature that we are foolish to try to change? Or is the attractiveness of these toys due to superficial features, especially their packaging, that send cultural signals about the toys' maleness or femaleness?

## The Rhinestone Gun and the GI Joe Teapot

One fascinating study[1] shows the power of marketing. The study was conducted with youngsters 3–7 years of age, who were asked to say whether boys or girls or both boys and girls would be more likely to play with particular toys. The following three toys were selected: a gun and holster (a traditionally male toy) (fig. 6.1), a tea set (a traditionally female toy) (fig. 6.2), and a ball (a "neutral" toy).

FIGURE 6.1    A Traditionally Male
Toy
A gun and holster

FIGURE 6.2    A Traditionally Female
Toy
A tea set

First, the researchers established that the kids considered certain attributes masculine and others feminine. For example, smooth and soft were feminine, whereas hard, sharp, and angular were masculine.

Then the researchers altered the appearance of the gun and holster and the tea set and asked whether the altered toys would be for girls, for boys, or for both sexes.

Specifically, the gun was modified to be purple and covered with rhinestones (fig. 6.3).

The tea set was altered to look dark and dirty and was covered with angular spikes (fig. 6.4).

What did the researchers find?

When the toys were altered to send out "boy" or "girl" signals, boys and girls thought the spiky tea set was for boys and the purple rhinestone gun was for girls!

Even when children are presented with familiar objects, guns and teapots, whose "gender typing" they know well, they are more likely

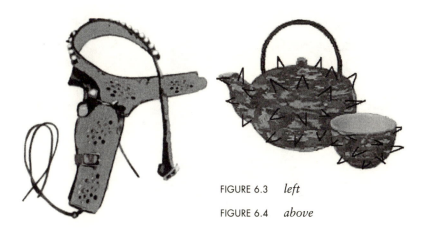

FIGURE 6.3    *left*

FIGURE 6.4    *above*

to base their decisions about whether the toys are for boys or girls on what "boy stuff " and "girl stuff" looks like than on any innate qualities of the objects themselves. These choices are learned and likely reflect the preferences of marketers and advertisers more than any basic gender differences. The power of marketing is abundantly clear.

In another study,[2] preschoolers were shown two groups of toys: a tool set (fig. 6.5) and a kitchen set. Half of the 61 children were told that the tool set was for boys and the kitchen set was for girls. The other half were not given these gendered labels for the toys. The children were also asked what they thought their mothers and fathers would say if they played with each of the toys. Would they say that it was good, bad, or that it didn't matter?

How much time did the boys play with the tools? Intriguingly, the answer depended on whether they were told anything about the toys and on their ideas about their fathers' reactions (fig. 6.6).

When they were told nothing about the toys, the boys spent about the same amount of time playing with the kitchen set as with the tools, regardless of their perceptions of their fathers' views about cross-gendered play. However, when the tools were labeled as being for boys, those who thought their fathers would consider cross-gendered

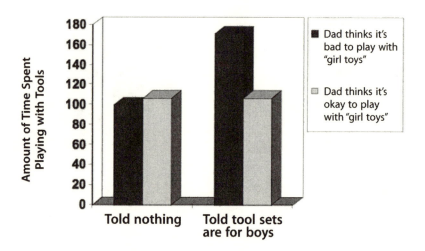

FIGURE 6.5

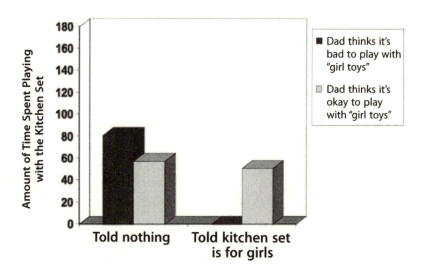

FIGURE 6.6

toy play "bad" spent significantly more time with the tools than those who thought their fathers would be less upset.

How much time did the boys play with the kitchen set? It's easy to see that boys liked playing with the kitchen set when it wasn't given a gender label or when they thought their fathers would think it was good or didn't matter if they played with it.

However, the situation was very different for the boys who perceived that their fathers would think that playing with the kitchen set was "bad." Those boys played far less with the kitchen set. In fact, when the kitchen set was labeled "for girls," *not one* of the boys who reported that their fathers would think cross-gender play was "bad" ever touched the kitchen set.

According to the kids, fathers didn't much care which toys their girls played with, and mothers weren't concerned about which toys boys *or* girls played with. Clearly, these boys' decisions about what toys they played with were very strongly influenced by which ones were labeled as "for boys" or "for girls," and by what they thought their fathers would think. A lot more is going on here than "innate" choices dictated by biology. Parents need to know that children take what they think seriously and may—rightly or wrongly—infer "gender" messages from their parents' behavior.

These messages are especially problematic today because, across the spectrum of gifts and toys, most retailers have retreated to a pink-and-blue world, aiming products at the sexes as if they really did come from different planets. After a unisex phase, large toy stores have returned to boy and girl aisles because they are more profitable.

"The gulf between His and Her sides looms like the parted Red Sea," writes Michael Kimmel,[3] a sociologist at the State University of New York, Stony Brook. "Woe to him who strolls inadvertently into Barbie-land from the land of the action figures. It's not simply those cute blue-and-pink blankets anymore. Everything is coded."

In the fall of 2009, we sent researcher Katie Plocheck on a scouting mission into the land of pink and blue. In an era when girls play sports, take advanced math classes, and show a strong interest in the sciences, Katie found herself traveling back in time to the 1950s.

I went to Toys R Us yesterday. I found the store to be extremely gendered. This included the sports and activities aisles, which would denote girls' bikes, hockey sticks, and toolboxes with a very bright pink. The same was true for Legos, which I always considered to be gender neutral. Girls now have a pink set that includes a house, flower pots, etc. In those sections where toys for girls were pink, the boys' toys stood out in deep contrast, such that there were no 'neutral toys.' The boys' bikes, sports items, and other activity toys were not a bright blue, but rather painted with army machinery, lighting bolts, and fast cars.

Overall, the store was laid out in a very gendered fashion as well. Aisle hangers that denoted what was on a particular aisle included such categories as "Building," "Action Figures," "Learning," and "Wheels" all of which included photos of boys on the aisle hangers. The only section that was exclusively female in the store was the "Home and Dress-Up" section, which of course included dollhouses, Barbies, cooking sets and dress-up clothes. The aforementioned "boy" aisles included no girl toys except for a couple of pink toys obviously made more feminine (pink tricycle, pink Little People—princess, marriage set, jewelry). In aisles like action figures, there were no girl counterparts.

The only somewhat gender-neutral aisles I found were the stuffed animals and the learning and game aisles. Some gendered divisions were apparent, but overall there were more items the same.

I also went to Target, and found very similar delineations in the toy section. Boys have many more options when it comes to colors: red, blue, green, yellow. Girls' items are always pink, unless they choose gender neutral or boys' toys. It was very obvious walking up to the toy section which were the boy and girl aisles, with games being the only neutral section.

We'd been watching this trend for several years. In 2005, in its newspaper supplement catalog, Toys "R" Us offered no pictures of girls on its sports page. Boys, meanwhile, were seen playing basketball, riding an arcade-style motorcycle, and playing an electronic hockey game. No girls were seen in two pages of action-figure toys or in two pages of cars and trucks. Two pages devoted to building toys featured boys playing with Legos, Tinkertoys, Lincoln Logs, and a huge "tube park."

In today's world, toys that teach skills like spatial tracking, causation, and compliance (important for engineering) are not being marketed to girls. Bob the Builder, a wonderful set of toys, could also have been named Jane the Builder, or some gender-free name like Leslie the Builder. The failure to do so creates a barrier that most parents find it hard to cross in picking out toys for their young daughters. Such marketing decisions create additional hurdles that parents have to leap if they want their girls to acquire important skills that they might not otherwise obtain.

## Toy Machismo?

Toy manufacturers are heavily focused on the "boy" market and, almost as an afterthought, shoehorn girls into what works for boys. "Toys Unfair: There's an Unending Variety of Toys for Boys, but Marketers Haven't Gotten Much Beyond Barbie and Baubles for Girls,"[4] rang one trade magazine headline. In terms of sheer dollars, the gender gap is enormous. Although girls represent almost 49 percent of U.S. children aged 4 to 12, only some $5.5 billion is spent on them annually out of about $17.5 billion total spent on toy marketing.

Some lay the blame for this asymmetry on a certain machismo in the toy business that carries over to the product lines, promotions, and total marketing mix. Others say that girls will play with "boys'" toys but not vice versa. So the logic goes, why spend millions to develop girl-centered products that will appeal to only half of the kids' market? Some say that parents are the problem; they are anxious about buying the "wrong" gendered toy for their children for fear that they will somehow damage their child's gender identity.

When it comes to action toys: motorbikes, scooters, pulleys, and so on, it's clear that we are in "boy" territory. These toys teach about spatial skills, balance, velocity, eye-hand coordination, and other science-related concepts. Girls are pictured (if at all) as passive observers, whereas boys are actively engaged in the science-learning projects.

In one toy catalog, girls were offered Cinderella Castle blocks (with a battery-powered waltz) and a cheap toddler block set. On a learn-and-create page, boys played with toy trains while girls seemed delighted with a "glitter dream dollhouse."

In a product list from Mattel aimed at young boys, the dominant theme was action and speed. Hot Wheels and Matchbox racing cars, pocket-sized die-cast four-wheel cars, were prominently featured. Matchbox cars have more realistic models, whereas Hot Wheels are more "far out," including tiny hot rod and "concept" cars. Amazingly, two Hot Wheels cars are sold somewhere in the world every second of the day!

Too often, toys and toy advertising make boys think they have to be tough and cool, athletic and stoic, say Lyn Mikel Brown, Sharon Lamb, and Mark Tappan[5] in *Packaging Boyhood*. This messaging starts early, with toddler T-shirts emblazoned with "Future All-Star" or "Little Champion." Worse, a new line of infant wear called Pimpfants even offers baby T-shirts emblazoned with "Pimp jr." and "My mother is a (expletive deleted)." Once-benign toys like Legos and Nerf have assumed a more aggressive profile with Lego Exo-Force Assault Tigers and the Nerf N-Strike Raider Rapid Fire CS-35 Dart Blaster. "That kind of surprised us," says one of the book's authors, Lyn Mikel Brown,[6] a professor of education and human development at Colby College. "What happened to Nerf? What happened to Lego?"

An example of viewing girls as merely "add-on" customers for boys' toys comes from Mattel and its effort to expand the Hot

Wheels market to girls. Mattel has introduced Polly Wheels, the first-ever toy cars designed exclusively for girls. Like Hot Wheels, they are pocket-sized, but unlike the boys' version, Polly Wheels come equipped with miniature drivers, who are female.

The cars are fruit scented and heavy into candy colors, such as "Splashin' Pink" and "Glitter Peach." Each one has a different look and smell coming out of the package. Mattel says the new line of cars for girls opens up numerous possibilities for the company. For example, the candy-and-glitter paint schemes could also lead to a line of matching makeup. "Girls want the glitter and glam," said a Mattel spokesperson.[7]

There's another big difference. The boys' version of Hot Wheels offers a set of tracks that allows the players to construct highways and racetracks, sparking creativity and teaching about spatial relations.

Not so for the Polly Wheels tracks. These tracks are preconstructed to go straight to a shopping mall. According to Mattel, with its "Race to the Mall" game: "On the top floor, there is a cool parking garage for Polly's car. Polly and her friends can go shopping, get their hair and make up done at the salon, or go get some food at the second level food court."

## All Dolled Up

If you want to start a firestorm of protest among toy manufacturers, just try calling an action figure a doll! Although there is no one definition of action figures, most agree that they are poseable character figurines, mostly made of plastic and often based upon a movie, comic book, video game, or television program. These action figures are usually marketed toward boys. The most popular ones represent traditional masculine traits—highly muscled, strong, and athletic. In contrast to action figures that have all or most of their clothes molded on, most redressable action figures (think Barbie) are sometimes referred to as action *dolls*.

In an attempt to lure boys to the doll market, in 1964 Hasbro coined the term "action figure" to market the company's G.I. Joe figure. Initially G.I. Joe featured changeable clothes with various uniforms to suit different purposes. Over the years, though, the "try-on" wardrobe was phased out. Too much like Barbie, with her passion for short red dresses and glitter shoes? Today, most boys' action figures are sold in a variety of different costumes, all of which are molded onto the figure.

One of the most hotly debated issues among action figure collectors is what is and what isn't an action figure? Why is it that calling an action figure a doll is such a no-no? Conversely, why is it such a faux pas to call Barbie an action figure? Both are small plastic characters designed for reenactment play by children. They can be posed and accessories can be placed in their hands. Yet most parents and children will insist that Barbie is a doll and not an action figure.

In toy-store catalogs, the dolls' page is, of course, for girls. There you can find items such as a Cinderella carriage, a Barbie primp-and-polish styling head for hairdos, a Hollywood party limo, and scores of Barbies. No boys are pictured.

Hot items in Toyland are the big-eyed Bratz dolls, sporting navel-baring tops, hooker boots, and miniskirts. The Bratz dolls are even more overtly sexual than Barbie. The toy industry—along with many parents—has noticed the so-called age-compression phenomenon.

Children are outgrowing traditional toys sooner. Not so long ago, girls up to age 12 played with Barbies. By 2000 such "tweens" were plugged into Britney Spears gyrating on MTV. This growing-up-fast syndrome may be one of the engines behind the success of the Bratz dolls, which are becoming more popular than Barbie.

In 2005 *Advertising Age*[8] reported: "Barbie has lost shelf space at major retailers and has been displaced by the edgy, hip-hop Bratz." Barbie's third-quarter sales were down 30 percent in the United States compared to the same period a year earlier, says the magazine.

"It's not the fact that children are learning about sex when they are young that is a problem," says Diane Levin,[9] a professor of child development at Wheelock College in Boston. "The problem is what today's sexualized environment is teaching them."

So what are kids learning and not learning when they spend their time playing with such toys? And are those the lessons we want to teach, especially to our daughters?

Kids are getting pulled into precocious sexual behavior for which they are not emotionally prepared. And girls are not learning the skills that will help them succeed in the high-tech world, which they will soon be entering. In contrast, boys are getting a leg up by having an array of toys, many of which teach them just those skills.

Playtime Teaches Serious Lessons

For years, conventional wisdom had it that the play of preschool children was all about having fun. Newer research reveals that children at play are actively engaged in serious learning.

One of the things they learn is that the world abides by stark and dominant gender roles. These toys teach girls who is in charge and which activities are "natural" and "good" for boys and girls.

These lessons are learned by age 4, according to Glenda Mac-Naughton,[10] associate professor of education at the University of Melbourne, who has conducted extensive research on equity issues in childhood. A rash of new studies shows that boys and girls as young as 3 or 4 years of age indeed do get the gender-difference message.

In the preschool world, boys are in charge, say a number of studies done by educators and social scientists. Boys appropriate the most-active play areas, and they tell girls what they can and can't do. Boys are learning that they are supposed to be the dominant sex and that they can treat girls as submissive and acquiescent.

From the toys and games of childhood, girls learn early that they should be accommodating so that when they grow up they will be desirable to the men they are expected to marry.

Here is how Adam, a middle-class 6-year-old Caucasian boy, who is well respected by the boys and girls in his kindergarten class, put it: "Look, boys are supposed to do boy things and girls, well, they do all those girly things. That is how it is! Boys play football. Girls are cheerleaders. And we aren't going to mess with it. That is final!"

By contrast, the real world for which these children are practicing is one in which most women will be in the workforce and most men will be expected to help raise families. Moreover, men will often be working with or for women.

Getting zipped into outmoded gender roles while they are still toddlers will only make children's lives more fraught with confusion and conflict as they grow up. And we are learning more and more about how the choices of adults, not the desires of kids, drive the toy market.

## Dora the Explorer

Sometimes, parents looking for toys that avoid gender stereotypes can indeed find good products. But even those products can morph into a shape dictated by the tyranny of pink and blue. The old maxim that boys would not play with "girl" toys or watch programs about girls was shattered by *Dora the Explorer*, the number one show on commercial television for kids ages 2 to 5, with retail sales of licensed goods to the tune of half a billion (yes, billion) dollars in 2005. Dora is an active Latina who loves adventures and appeals equally to boys and girls; more than half of kids between ages 2 and 5 who have access to Nickelodeon watch the show.

Instead of using gender as a premise for the character, the creators relied on Harvard professor Howard Gardner's multiple intelligences theory, which recognizes that preschoolers solve problems by utilizing many forms of intelligence.

Dora wears an outdoorsy outfit of shorts and shirt, calls out, "Let's go!" as she takes off on adventures with a friendly monkey, solving problems as she goes.

But bloggers Lyn Mikel Brown and Sharon Lamb,[11] authors of *Packaging Girlhood*, began to notice some problems in Dora's World. They noticed that Dora was getting—well, a tad more like Barbie. They also noted a proliferation of products like Dora's Magic Talking Kitchen, and Dora Princess, and noticed a "cute flower lip gloss, the *pinkified* look."

Even more worrisome, Mattel bought the franchise for a "tween" Dora. One of the first changes the company made was to have Dora give up her shirt and shorts for a miniskirt. Mattel decided that Dora would become a city dweller—no more outdoor adventures.

Parents protested, but the company said, "The brand captures girls' existing love of Dora and marries it with the fashion doll play and online experiences older girls love." Mattel seems to have "forgotten" that boys as well as girls loved Dora.

Mattel also seems to have forgotten that generations of young girls and boys will no longer have the "old" Dora as a wonderful role model. It's also worth noting that marketers had no problem with allowing other children's favorites—Elmo, Linus, Barney—to avoid the "growing up" that Dora is being forced to undergo.

Brown and Lamb worry about "the cute sexy way that marketers sell maturity to girls—the sassy wink, the long flowing hair, the thin waist, the turned out hip pose of practiced lingerie models." What's next? Dora the Cheerleader? Dora the Fashionista with stylish purse and stilettos? Dora the Pop Star with Hoppin' Dance Club and "Juice" Bar? We can expect it all, because that's what passes as "tween" in the toy department these days.

Disneyland

Moviemakers also have a powerful effect on kids, both directly through the films themselves and indirectly through the toys and accessories that are marketed as tie-ins. Disney movies have been a huge favorite of the younger set. And, indeed, something newsworthy is happening at Disney!

Disney is now producing more rounded male and female characters. A warm and loving father-son relationship is at the heart of *Finding Nemo*, and Disney took a giant step away from passive females who need to be rescued in *Mulan*. *Newsweek*[12] noted that unlike previous heroines in Disney's animations, Mulan "doesn't look like a Barbie doll, she doesn't dream about a prince and she certainly doesn't hang around waiting to be rescued." As a woman warrior, she captures the trust and respect of all those around her.

More recently, as *Salon*[13] notes, in *The Princess and the Frog,* the main character, Tiana, "takes the princess role a step further—she's not just Disney's first African-American to wear the crown, she's the first one with a regular job. (Unless you count Mulan's gig as a warrior.)"

Still, the toy industry has been slow to move away from stereotypes, and parental pressure is very much needed. The more parents (and kids) respond to healthy toys and shows like Dora, the better things will get for all kids.

# 7 THE MORE AGGRESSIVE SEX?

Are boys naturally the more aggressive sex? No, this is not a trick question. It turns out that the answer depends on how you define aggression, on the person of whom you ask the question, and on the setting in which the question is asked.

For a long time, we've simply assumed that males are aggressive while females are, in the words of the old poem, "sugar and spice and everything nice." We have focused so intently on male aggression that we assume it's omnipresent, and so we often ignore female aggression, assuming that it isn't there.

What's the real truth?

To find out, you have to ask the basic question, What is aggression?

It seems simple at first glance, but that is hardly the case. We can all agree that a physical attack on another person is aggression. But what about verbal accusations? Or public criticism? Or rough contact in sports? Or bullying and gossip? Even if we agree to call behaviors that result in physical or psychological harm aggression, we do not necessarily mean that they are equivalent. Some are intended to cause harm; others are not.

If you define aggression as rough-and-tumble play, the actions that fill the bill will be different than if you define aggression as an expression of intimate friendly play, or as injurious assault. If you ask a child's peers to answer the question, the answer will be different from the answer you'd get if you ask the child herself. Moreover, if you ask a child from a non-aggressive culture the question, the answer will be different from the one you'd receive if you ask a child from a culture where there is a high level of aggression. In addition, if you had asked that question in the United States in the 1950s the answer would have been different than it would be today.

Aggression never occurs in a vacuum. Whether it's a full-fledged adult bar fight, a couple of kids laughing and shoving each other on a playground, a hockey player blocking her opponent in a game, or a bully taunting another child, the situation is crucial. Although not much attention is paid to "situational variation" in aggression, there is a growing body of research in the United States and across cultures suggesting that it is the key element. In fact, the context in which aggression occurs is *more important* than sex differences in explaining its causes.

This may sound jarring, because we have all read for years about studies showing that school-age boys exhibit more aggressive behavior than their female peers, Those studies, it turns out, may have been wrongly interpreted. The dominant, bullying boys grab the attention of researchers and skew the results. Psychologists Claudia Fry and Siegfried Hoppe-Graff, of the University of Heidelberg,[1] conclude, in their observations of nursery school children, that notable sex differences in "bullying" were due to the behavior of a minority of boys; the majority displayed the same range of bullying as the girls did.

It seems that researchers, like the rest of us, assume that boys will act in certain ways and focus on those behaviors, paying less attention to the more numerous non-aggressive behaviors that are more typical of most boys, most of the time. This new observation echoes that of Barrie Thorne[2] in her groundbreaking 1993 book on elementary

106

school children, *Gender Play*. She observed that the dominant boys were the ones who held the researchers' attention; boys who were less aggressive were "not noticed." With this bias operating, the picture we get of boys and aggression is surely distorted.

We need to take a closer look at the data on gender differences in aggression and ask a very important question: Why the excessive focus on aggression in children? Considering all the attention paid, you would imagine that such behavior was rampant, that it accounted for a high percentage of all young children's behavior.

Not true! Across cultures, the overall number of aggressive or antagonistic behaviors of children is relatively low.[3] Indeed, such behavior made up less than 10 percent of the children's total social acts.

So, one category of preschool children's behavior—aggression—dominates research and concern, yet accounts for only a tiny percentage of all behavior. Why does aggression, a relatively infrequent behavior, dominate research and concern?

Maybe it's because we are so wedded to a male stereotype in which aggression is key that we over-focus on aggression in boys. Michael Gurian[4] goes so far as to suggest that boys should be given Nerf baseball bats with which to hit things so they can release tension during class.

Or maybe it's because a few violent acts by young males—such as the Columbine shootings—dominate the mass media. Those interested in perpetuating the belief in large gender differences locked on to one area of behavior in which some gender difference can be demonstrated, while ignoring a whole range of other behavior unlikely to show dramatic differences.

Rough-and-Tumble Play

When we see a couple of young boys tussling like bear cubs, what do we think? Probably that this kind of play prefigures the aggression that is "natural" to adult males. One of the most persistent gender differences seems to be a greater predilection for rough-and-tumble (R&T) play among young males, human and non-human alike, as well as across various human cultures. R&T play is defined by some but not all scientists as aggression; however, like other terms, that word covers a wide range of behavior.

These generalizations, of course, refer to group differences, which mask considerable variation within sex. Many girls engage in more R&T play than many boys. Such broad statements do not permit us to say anything about the behavior of individual boys and girls. For example, the "tomboy" is well known to every parent who has ever taken his or her child to a playground as well as to every primary school teacher.

Traditionally, parents and teachers looked with dismay on any displays of aggression by girls, while the "boys will be boys" adage caused grown-ups to look the other way when boys scuffled. That situation is changing as more and more girls play contact sports at earlier ages. Still, girls' behavior is more culturally constrained than boys' behavior, and kids know who's watching and what those "others" expect of them. They act accordingly. Here is another example showing how the situations in which children are observed may be more important in predicting aggressive behavior than the child's sex.

Some studies show[5] that when preschoolers (average age 4 years) are closely supervised by adults, their behavior tends to adhere to the stereotype for their sex. Boys exhibit more playful physical assault, wrestling, and rough-and-tumble play, whereas girls exhibit more cooperative play—for example, waiting their turn in line and taking part in verbal games.

It's easy to see how such studies underscore common notions that given identical environments, girls and boys will engage in very different play patterns.[6] We assume that girls' play involves much more verbal structure and rules, while boys' involves more unrestrained roughhousing.

However, when kids are not so closely supervised—in indoor or outdoor nursery school settings—girls' behavior is far less constrained and they may be as aggressive as boys. Free from the eyes of adults, girls, it seems, can let their high spirits and their assertive instincts have free rein. Psychologist Janet DiPietro observes that "girls' and boys' behavior may be more a function of the particular context of their play activities than of intrinsic gender attributes." In other words, who's watching is more important than who's playing.

In fact, how much aggression kids actually show depends heavily on parents' and teachers' approval and modeling, the behavior of peers, media images, and marketing pitches to kids. While boys are often rewarded for their physical aggression, girls are punished more severely for such behavior. By the same token, girls get more leeway for verbal aggression.

One dramatic experiment showed how much aggressive behavior depends on what children see in adults. The study was done in 1961 by noted psychologist Albert Bandura,[7] of Stanford University, and the results are considered among the most important breakthroughs in children's social learning.

In this landmark study, children were exposed to adults, male and female, who modeled aggressive and non-aggressive behavior. The adults interacted with a "Bobo" doll—one of those inflatable figures you can hit and it bounces right back up.

The adult models demonstrated behavior that was unusually aggressive both physically and verbally toward the Bobo doll. For example, the model laid the Bobo doll on its side, sat on it, and punched it repeatedly in the nose. The adult then raised the Bobo doll, picked up a mallet and struck the Bobo on the head. The adult also tossed the doll up in the air and kicked it around the room. These physical acts were interspersed with such verbal responses as "Sock him in the nose," "Throw him in the air," and "Kick him."

After the adult left the room, those children who had watched adults, especially males, model aggressive behavior, subsequently exhibited a good deal of physical and verbal aggression toward Bobo that was substantially identical to that of the adult model (fig. 7.1).

In contrast, youngsters who were exposed to non-aggressive adult models only rarely performed aggressive behavior. And when kids who were not exposed to any adult models were alone with the Bobo, *neither* boys nor girls demonstrated aggressive behavior.

The graph below shows how children responded when they witnessed very aggressive male behavior toward the Bobo doll. Boys and girls in the aggressive condition with a male model exhibited

FIGURE 7.1

more physically aggressive behavior than boys and girls in the non-aggressive condition.

However, the effect was much stronger for the boys. Modeling of physically aggressive behavior by males had an especially strong impact on the boys (fig. 7.2).

What about verbal aggression? The greatest amount of verbal imitation occurred among girls who witnessed an aggressive female model (fig. 7.3). The results for the boys were similar, but less striking.

Overall, this study provides strong support for the effect of social learning on children's aggressive play. It appears that boys' physical aggression was more affected when they watched an aggressive male model. In contrast, girls' verbal aggression was more affected when they witnessed an aggressive female model.

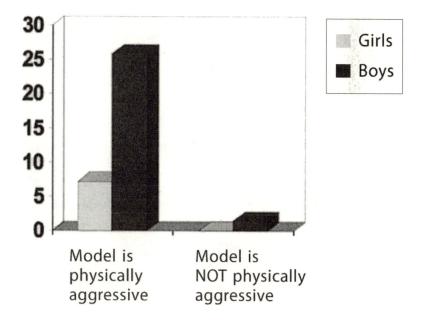

FIGURE 7.2    Physical Aggression, Male Model

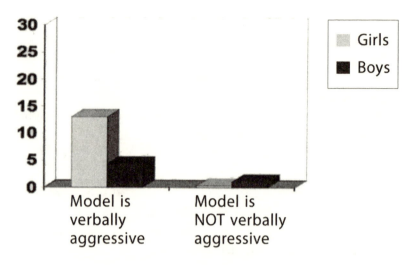

FIGURE 7.3   Verbal Aggression, Female Model

Is overt aggressive behavior a good test of innate gender differences? Not really. Kids pick up cues—maybe even subtle ones—from parents and others about how to channel their aggressive feelings. It's not that boys are innately wired to act out physically—children's aggression is shaped by their early learning environment.

It appears that kids at even very early ages are fully aware of society's views of appropriate behavior for girls and boys. When this study was done, little boys were more physically aggressive and engaged in more risky behaviors than did little girls. It demonstrated that gender-difference stereotypes have an early and powerful effect in shaping a range of social behaviors that channel boys and girls into different paths with lifelong consequences.

Little girls are especially affected. Girls often get the message that they are supposed to heal, not hurt, and when they behave aggressively they may fear that they will be punished more severely than their brothers. The women these girls grow up to be internalize this message. But what happens when women think nobody's watching? A study conducted by two Princeton psychologists[8] shed some surprising light on this question.

They asked a random sample of 84 college-age men and women to play a video game in which they would drop bombs on an opponent, and in turn would be bombed themselves. Study participants were told that they had been matched with someone at another terminal in the room but they would never know who that person was. The researchers knew the identities of only half the group. In the "unknown" group, both gender and names were hidden; in the "known" group, participants wore name tags and were visible to the experimenters.

The results were revealing. Being observed changes women's behavior—but not men's. When their identity was known, males dropped significantly more bombs than females did. But when their identity was unknown, females dropped *more* bombs than the men. Granted anonymity, women were significantly more aggressive than men. Indeed, they bombed their opponents back to the Stone Age—a most unladylike way to behave. As you can see in figure 7.4, men didn't behave much differently whether they were watched or not—because there are few social constraints on men's macho behavior.

After the game, participants were asked in a face-to-face situation with the researcher to report their own aggressiveness and the number of bombs they dropped. The men described themselves, accurately, as aggressive. But the women reported themselves as having behaved less aggressively than they had. If the study had accepted only the women's self-reports, it would have reflected the common wisdom that women are naturally less aggressive than men. Apparently when the aggressive students, whose gender had previously been anonymous to the researchers, were revealed as girls, they presented themselves as stereotypically female—that is, as not aggressive. They acted very much like the preschoolers in the Heidelberg study we discussed earlier.

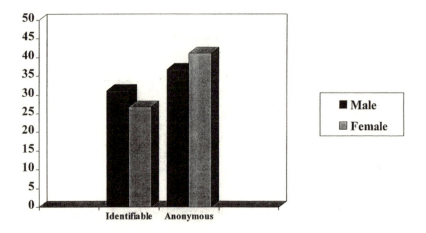

FIGURE 7.4    Effects of Anonymity and Subject Sex on Number of Bombs Dropped
*Source*: Adapted from Lightdate and Prentice (1994), Study 2, Number of Bombs Dropped in Round Two.

## Models Make a Difference

So it's important for parents to model appropriate assertive behavior for children. Sticking up for yourself is an important trait to learn. Both boys and girls need to know they can be strong verbally and sometimes physically. (If a kid grabs your daughter's toy, she needs to be able to grab it back and strongly assert her right to it.) Despite trendy recent claims that parents don't matter much, experiments like the one described above show that parents do indeed have a big impact on kids.

New research validates the power of parents' behavior. Psychologist Steve Biddulph[9] says that from early infancy, boys are spoken to less and that as they grow, they are disciplined more harshly, "with mothers tending to hit boys more often than they do girls." Mothers supported boys' aggressive behavior three times more often than

114

they did aggressive behavior among girls. These reactions are paramount in developing aggressive behavior.

Play Fighting

Yet another view of children's aggression is voiced by psychologist Anne Humphreys,[10] of the University of Durham, England, who thinks we too often confuse rough-and-tumble play with aggression. Humphreys disassociates R&T from aggression, referring to it instead as "play fighting." She asserts that R&T indeed takes place among boys more than girls, but *only* when it comes to contact play (fighting), as opposed to non-contact play, such as chasing, which boys and girls engage in almost equally.

And play fighting doesn't have the simple script of aggressor and victim. Humphreys says that when R&T occurs through the "mutual consent of engaged actors," it includes no victim/victimizer dynamic, which is an integral part of true aggression.

Whether play has "rules" or not can affect gender differences in aggression. Gender differences generally do exist among kids aged 7 to 11. But when kids play such games as Red Rover or King of the Hill that have clear rules, even though they involve some rough-and-tumble play, girls and boys behave similarly. Rules become another "situation" that shapes behavior, perhaps more so than gender.

A Special Form of Intimate Play

Here's a really intriguing question: Have we completely misinterpreted rough-and-tumble play by seeing it as evidence of an innate capacity for aggression by boys? Could it be something else altogether? Yes, say some researchers. They believe R&T occurs in the context of friendship. Rather than being a form of aggression, Tom Reed and Mac Brown,[11] of the University of South Carolina, say, R&T provides a context for "the declaration of friendship." In this view, boys are not the more aggressive sex; rather, they engage in "different types of intimate play." R&T gives boys an acceptable medium for being physically close in cultural or social environments that otherwise discourage such behavior. Boys who display the kind of contact that's perfectly okay for girls, like holding hands, risk taunts and mockery. But through R&T, boys can showcase their care and intimacy for one another. For example, in the context of R&T, "hanging on" and walking arm in arm are considered perfectly acceptable behaviors. One boy in the study said, "They have their arms around each other [because] they are friends."

Given that R&T has generally been seen as a form of aggression typically exhibited by young males, little research attention has been paid to R&T in young females. Perhaps with these new understandings of the meaning of R&T, more research will address the behavior of young girls in this respect.

Overall, our understanding of rough-and-tumble play is changing.

Michelle Tannock,[12] of the University of Nevada, tends to focus on the play aspect of R&T. She doesn't see it as worrisome or pathological; rather she views it as a "multi-dimensional, developmental activity expressed through a variety of forms and actions that takes on an increasingly important role as children move into their preschool years." Tannock found that both educators and children in child-care facilities were ambivalent about rough-and-tumble play. Although the young children she studied said that they were not allowed to engage in R&T, each child was observed engaging in it.

So how should teachers and parents look at rough-and-tumble play? Should it be discouraged as leading to harmful aggression or encouraged as natural and sometimes even useful behavior?

The new research suggests a benign view of R&T. Children who engage in rough-and-tumble play are learning to make judgments about their physical abilities, how to respond to others, and how their playmates respond to them. They are also learning about self-control, compassion, boundaries, and their own abilities in relation to other players.

Rough-and-tumble play is normal—and now more girls are involved in it as well. We should not see it as a precursor of male aggression or as totally inappropriate for girls—rather we can view it as a stage kids go through in managing their relationships. And as a chance for boys to be physically companionable.

Too much worry about girls engaging in rough-and-tumble could harm girls in the long run. If we block all rough-and-tumble play for young girls, where will they take their need for physicality and their need to learn the boundaries between assertion and true aggression? Too often girls turn early to verbal aggression—which, unlike rough-and-tumble play, is always meant to wound. Some kids may become "Mean Girls" because they weren't allowed to use the energies in R&T play when they were younger.

Of course teachers and parents do need to intervene when rough-and-tumble play becomes dangerous or turns into bullying. And preschool children who manifest severe problem behavior are at high risk and in need of professional services.

How can teachers and parents distinguish rough-and-tumble play from more serious aggression? Look for the "play face," Michelle Tannock says. When kids are really serious about hurting one another, you can see it in the intensity—one might even say the hardness—in their faces. But when kids are just having fun, the joy and high spirits can be read in their expressions.

Looking at rough-and-tumble play, we tend to confuse "correlation" and "causation." As we've noted, all too often in sex-difference research, leaps are made that don't actually pan out. For example, psychologist Carol Jacklin[13] notes that if we see boys being more physically aggressive than girls in the schoolyard, we assume that the difference is biological and immutable, "though neither equation is necessarily correct." This confusion is a major driver for the perpetuation of gender stereotypes.

If we see men but no women engaging in some activity, we assume that their gender causes their behavior. In the days when only men were hired as police officers, only males prosecuted crimes in the courtroom, and only men flew in space, we thought that women would never do such things, because "nature" destined them for other, quieter paths. Now that women run city police departments, Sally Ride has soared in space, and the courts are filled with tough lady prosecutors, we can see that our old ideas were flawed. Clearly, "nature" had nothing to do with men's monopoly in these areas.

## Context Matters

Underscoring the critical role of "situation," Tom Reed and Mac Brown, of the University of South Carolina, say there are as many different definitions of play as there are cultures in the world, and "play is more a function of culture than it is a developmental process." A cross-cultural perspective is important because the severe sanctions on aggression in some cultures, especially for young girls, may mask their "natural" aggressive tendencies. Such sanctions may vary from one part of the world to another. For example, we were talking recently to a teenager from China about the demure behavior that many Chinese girls display in the classroom. Yes, she said, but you should see them with their friends, just hanging out. In that setting, the girls are boisterous and assertive in ways they are not in the classroom, where deference to the teacher's authority is expected,

A tough female district attorney in the United States will almost certainly behave much differently than a housewife in a traditional rural village in the Middle East, where women's activities are limited and aggression is severely punished. At the same time, in a culture where boys do a lot of caretaking of young children, they will be less aggressive than boys in a culture where such caretaking among boys is regarded as "sissy stuff."

In both instances, it's not the gender that's the vital difference, but the culture. Indeed, the newest cross-cultural research finds that in regard to aggression, culture is more important than sex.

Times Are Changing

Girls aren't so "girly" anymore.

Perhaps it began with early female action figures. Perhaps with *Charlie's Angels*. Or maybe with scores of elementary girls playing soccer, or with older girls playing contact sports at elite levels. Most likely we will never know exactly how or when it became okay to talk about female aggression—female-to-female aggression and female-to-male aggression. Whatever its origins, this new narrative is challenging the once omnipresent scenario of the male violent aggressor–passive female victim scenario. It is now increasingly acceptable to talk openly about female aggression and to conduct serious research on this topic.[14] We now know that women-on-women aggression is far from rare and that women are often the initiators of male-female aggression.[15] Surveys of U.S. households[16] have found rates of wife-to-husband violence "remarkably similar:" to those of husband-to-wife violence. And an early cross-cultural survey (Rohner 1976) did not find that men were significantly more aggressive than women.[17] Aggression, as opposed to anger, conveys an intent to hurt or harm and can be expressed physically, verbally, or by withdrawing. There is general agreement that men exhibit higher levels of physical aggression than women, but the differences are small to moderate. After a thorough review of the literature on who initiates violence in couples, Murray Straus, of the University of New Hampshire, reports: "It is painful to have to recognize the high rate of domestic assaults by women. All six major studies which have investigated this topic found that women initiate violence in a large proportion of the cases." For example, of the 495 couples in a 1985 National Family Violence Survey for whom one or more assaults were reported by a woman respondent, the man was the only violent partner in 25. 9 percent of the cases, the woman was the only one to be violent in 25. 5 percent of the cases, and both were violent in 48.6 percent of the cases. Of 446 women who reported that they were involved in violent relationships, their partners struck the first blow in 42 percent of the cases. The women hit first in 53 percent of the cases, and they could not remember who hit first in the remaining cases.

The great difference here is that women are far more often seriously hurt or killed than men. A woman may start a fight with a slap, which is mildly painful to the man, but he retaliates by punching her and throwing her against the wall, breaking her jaw.

But it is important to recognize that although men are predominantly the murderers, rapists, and batterers in human society, relatively few men ever perpetrate these acts. If you discount the extremely violent behavior of those few, the behavior of most men resembles that of most women.

## Different Strokes for Different Folks

As noted, for too long we have failed to question the violent male aggressor–passive female victim scenario.[18]

Finnish researcher Kaj Björkqvist suggests that it is nonsensical to frame our questions about sex differences in terms of "more" or "less." His studies are based on the supposition that "there is no reason to believe that females should be less hostile and less prone to get into conflicts than males." Instead, he and his colleagues assume that boys and girls, and men and women, develop different styles of aggressive behavior.

This turns out to be true. Looking at boys as pint-size Conans and girls as passive little victims is *not* the real story.[19] The Finnish researchers investigated three types of aggressive behavior (physical, verbal, and indirect) among 8-, 11-, and 15-year-olds in Finland, Israel, and Poland.

If verbal and physical aggression are forms of direct aggression, what is indirect aggression? One answer comes from the hit movie *Mean Girls*, in which high schools girls made each other's lives miserable. Indirect aggression is social manipulation, attacking the target in circuitous ways. For example, girls are more likely to exclude newcomers from a group than boys are. Also, in one study[20] of British schools, girls exceeded boys in indirect bullying—insulting and threatening by gesture or statement.

Across nations, ethnic groups, and age groups, indirect aggression was used most by girls, verbal aggression was the second-most-used style, and physical aggression was used least often.

Among boys, a different pattern emerged. Indirect aggression was, in all ages, the least-used aggressive style. Physical and verbal aggression was used equally often at ages 8 and 11, while by the age of 15 verbal aggression had surpassed physical aggression and was the most-used style.

Victimization

So who is most often victimized by forms of aggression? At the age of 8, girls were most often victims of all three styles of aggression, but by 11, they were significantly more often victims of verbal than indirect aggression and of indirect than of physical aggression. At age 15, girls were most often victims of indirect aggression and least often of physical aggression. The "mean girls" were emerging. The proportion of physical aggression diminished consistently with age, while indirect aggression increased dramatically from age 11 to age 15.

In all age groups, boys were significantly less victimized by indirect than by physical or verbal aggression. At the age of 8, they were equally often victims of physical and verbal aggression, while at the ages of 11 and 15, they were significantly more often victims of verbal than of physical aggression.

So if you only look at physical aggression, boys corner the market. This limited view can lead to claims like this one in a textbook on cross-cultural social psychology, that there is an "almost universal tendency" for males to be more aggressive than females.

But use a broader lens that includes indirect and verbal aggression, and the picture changes. Some studies[21] show that girls are more aggressive than boys, using indirect aggression in their conflicts with others.

## The New American Girl

Girls, traditionally raised to be more passive than boys, are indeed becoming more aggressive, according to Professor James Garbarino,[22] of Loyola University, the author of *See Jane Hit*. Traditional cultural messages that girls are not pushy or violent are being diluted by images in the popular media—like *Buffy the Vampire Slayer* and *Lara Croft: Tomb Raider*—that portray women as aggressive,

"In the past . . . the clear message has been that girls don't hit," said Professor Garbarino. "However, that has changed as we see more girls on TV who hit and are more aggressive generally. Consequently, we are seeing more aggression in girls."

On the negative side, there's increasing violence among troubled girls. But overall, the news is good. As Professor Garbarino says, "Girls in general are evidencing a new assertiveness and physicality that . . . is evident in their participation in sports, in their open sensuality, in their enjoyment of 'normal' aggression that boys have long enjoyed in rough-and-tumble play, and in the feeling of confidence that comes with physical prowess and power." For example, consider the following:

At age 4, girls are nearly as likely to use physical aggression as boys—
24 percent versus 27 percent.

Thirty years ago, TV violence stimulated aggression in boys but not
girls. Today, the effects are equally apparent for boys and girls.

A study of aggression of 11,000 6- to 12-year-old kids found that
while girls started out being somewhat less aggressive, they soon
caught up and often exceeded boys in hostile behavior.

Garbarino puts it bluntly: "The fact is, children—boys and girls—
start out aggressive and for the first three years of life, boys and girls
are almost equally aggressive." He says, of one five-year-old girl,
"In addition to being the apple of my eye, Sally is a very aggressive
child. Although she is not as aggressive as some of the boys in her
class, I have seen her push other kids down to the ground, hit other
children and even slap her father. In all this, Sally's behavior in no
way seems surprising or shocking, though a generation ago, it would
have been."

## Risk-Taking Behavior

Taking appropriate risks is part of a healthy life—since simply being
alive involves some degree of risk. The issue is separating unwise,
unsafe risk from actions that give kids confidence and self-esteem.

There is no evidence of sex difference in risk taking in infancy.
Rather, a difference emerges between 2 and 3 years of age and peaks
during the teen and young adult years.

From very early on, parents may discourage girls from taking risks
by routinely underestimating their daughters' abilities. In one study,
11-month-old babies were allowed to crawl down a carpeted slope
that had adjustable angles. First, the mothers were asked to adjust
the ramp to the angle they thought their babies would be capable
of crawling down. Then the kids were turned loose. It turned out

that boys and girls didn't differ when it came to the steepness of the slopes they crawled down. In fact, the girl babies tended to be a bit more daring. But the mothers' expectations were all wrong. In line with the stereotype, they thought the boys would be more venturesome and the girls more reticent. They thought their daughters would avoid the steep slopes, while they expected their boys would be fearless.

This intriguing study reveals how mothers start to underestimate their girls' physical ability at an early age. It also helps explain why mothers are quicker to intervene when they perceive that their daughters are doing something "risky."

Mothers of boys are slower to intervene than mothers of girls when their children climb too high or swing too fast. Other studies find that fathers and mothers are more tolerant of daughters' expressions of fear than sons', just as boys are discouraged from crying more often than girls are. And in the popular media, there is no end to the contrasts between brave male children and more cautious female children.[23] While girls these days eagerly hurl their snowboards towards the sky, crash into the boards at ice hockey rinks and dangle from rocks perched halfway up a mountain, males still have a decided edge in risk-taking.

Taking risks and coming through OK can shore up confidence. Women—even those who are as able as men—can come up short in this department. It takes confidence to ask for a promotion, to be the first to answer a challenging question in class or to defend your position on an important issue on the job.

In general, girls are becoming more assertive, and that's a good thing. In recent years, gender differences in risk-taking may be waning. Before 1980, the male advantage was clear. Since then, the gap has narrowed. Girls appear to be dropping their aversion to risk, or possibly, boys are hearing the messages about safety beamed constantly from the media and from parents. Most likely, both are true.

Girls are also competing more in the classroom, and by stepping up to the plate this way, they may be raising the level of their classmates. Girls seem to respond positively when they have high-achieving peers.[24] This may be a new phenomenon. Not too long ago it wasn't "cool" for girls to be smart; in fact girls often hid their successes because of fear of rejection. But things are different now. The most popular girls in the class may also be high achievers. When girls claim their success, it enhances their sense of competence and motivates them to take on greater challenges.

The message to parents is that you don't have to worry about girls' new assertiveness, unless that behavior is spilling over into violence or other antisocial actions, such as extreme "mean girl" behavior. Yet some parents worry, thinking that aggression in girls is unnatural. After all, many experts argue that boys' behavior is destined to be aggressive because of the male hormone testosterone. But parents and teachers will be surprised to know that between the ages of 7 months and 10 years, boys and girls do not differ in levels of testosterone.

"We should welcome the New American Girl's unfettered asser-tiveness and physicality," argues Professor Garbarino. "We should appreciate her athletic accomplishments, like the way she stands up for herself, and applaud her straightforward appreciation of herself as a physical being."

# 8 CARING

We've come along way, baby! (Or maybe, we've come a long way, dude!)

The familiar refrain is typically used to highlight progress that women have made toward shedding harmful stereotypes. As we will see, it is equally apt when applied to new understandings of the capacity of boys and grown men to nurture.

The stereotype of the distant dad is a staple of American mythology. The novel *The Man in the Gray Flannel Suit*[1] portrayed the 1950s man, consumed by his need to climb the corporate ladder in an effort to establish his masculine identity. Caring and nurture were not his concern; his wife was there to handle those aspects of life. The movie based on the novel was a box office hit, testifying to how well it resonated with many 1950s Americans. (As an illustration of its staying power, the book was reissued in 2002 with an introduction by author Jonathan Franzen.)

Even a whiff of domesticity in that era could brand a man as a wimp. One of the pop icons of the era, James Dean, graphically portrayed male angst. In the film *Rebel Without a Cause*, Dean's character's juvenile delinquency is clearly attributed to his father's wearing an apron. Psychologist Joseph Pleck[2] notes of that scene, in which Dean recoils after seeing his father washing the dishes, "World War II's returning hero had been transformed into a henpecked husband whose son holds him in contempt."

Some went so far as to assert that men were, by their nature, simply incapable of nurturing. In the 1970s, the influential psychoanalyst Nancy Chodorow[3] argued that while mothers teach their daughters to nurture and form a close bond with them, they push their sons away to allow them to separate and form a masculine identity. With their early connections to their mothers severed, men turn to the impersonal world of work and public life, their caring capacities having been thoroughly repressed.

They are unable to nurture, even if they want to.

Some conservatives, notably David Blankenhorn,[4] in his oft-cited book *Fatherless America*, have argued vigorously that men are not "natural" parents in the way that mothers are. He says that the correct role for fathers is to be providers to the family and "pals" to their children, but not primary caregivers.

This portrait of men (and boys) has had amazing staying power. Is it correct? In a word, no. Considerable research, some of it done in this country, some of it cross-cultural, paints a dramatically different picture of male nurturance.

Starting with very young boys, evidence that males are uncaring, unemotional, and non-nurturant is hard to come by. Quite the opposite! Babies, male and female, are naturally tuned in to caring and nurture. And children relate not only to humans but also to objects that represent caring and security.

### Linus's Blanket

The term "transitional object" was coined by famous British pediatrician-turned-psychoanalyst Donald Winnicott.[5] Infants evolve from complete dependence on their mothers to relative independence via attachment to their transitional objects. That's why it's traumatic to the child to take these objects away.

We all know what a transitional object is even though we probably know it by a different name. Babies usually start using these objects, often a blanket or a stuffed animal, at around 4 to 6 months of age. Typically children cuddle, love, or even mangle their object. Most children have a transitional object. According to Richard Passman,[6] a psychologist at the University of Wisconsin, Milwaukee, up to 60 percent of children in the United States have some sort of security blanket during childhood.

Infants and toddlers can easily become upset by the absence of their primary caregiver, typically their mother. Providing the child with a soft object such as a teddy bear or blanket (i.e., a transitional object) can encourage them to transfer affections to that object and thus become more independent and less clinging to their primary caretaker.

Through his research on the effects of security blankets on child development, Passman has found no negative or lasting effects—but many positive ones. Apparently all children, boys and girls alike, respond to the warmth and softness of these objects and seem to be consoled by them. Interestingly, Passman said that although he looked for gender differences in all of his data, he found none. Young boys and girls are equally likely to become attached to their security blankets and are equally comforted by them when the children are in moderately stressful situations.

According to theory, these objects enable the child to maintain a fantasy bond with the mother (or primary caretaker) as she increasingly separates for longer and longer periods of time. Thus, for example, the transitional object is important at bedtime and at other separations. As children develop, their needs for transitional objects change but are still apparent. Among toddlers, comfort objects may take the form of a blanket, a stuffed animal, a favorite toy, or even a musical toy. The object may also be the subject of the child's fantasies; for example, when a teddy bear is spoken to, hugged, or punished, it becomes a tool for practicing interaction with the external world. Playing with the transitional object provides a pathway to the child's independence.

Transitional objects are often retained even among primary school children. The tendency to hold on to transitional objects made its way into one of the country's most loved and well-read comic strips, *Peanuts*. Lucy is bothered by her younger brother Linus's addiction to his security blanket and she wants him to stop it. In one strip, she even cuts the blanket up so that she can steal and hide it. She once made a kite out of it and "accidentally" let go of it. Another time she buried the blanket, causing a frantic Linus to dig up almost the entire neighborhood before it was found.

A little boy we know wandered mournfully around his house trying to find his best friend. "Elmo, where are you, Elmo?" he kept repeating, while his Muppet friend did a stint in the washer-dryer. He was overjoyed when Elmo emerged all dry and fluffy.

Donald Winnicott, who worked during the mid-1900s, might not have imagined how important these objects are to so many children today who, as a consequence of divorce settlements, military deployments, or parents who travel for work, spend part of every week away from their primary caretaker. Boys and girls alike are distraught at such times unless they have with them their blanket, stuffed animal, or whatever their transitional object may be.

Strikingly, none of the theoretical or empirical studies[7] on transitional objects makes any mention of gender differences in children's need for or attachment to these objects.

Boys and Girls and Caring

A hallmark of U.S. toy marketing is that girls want to play with dolls, but boys never do. Dolls, it is thought, give a girl the opportunity to express her innate caring nature and play out her future maternal role. From this perspective, it is "natural" that boys would shun dolls. This bit of wisdom is never challenged, even though it requires a tortured definition of "dolls" to make it credible.

What is a doll? Is a stuffed animal a doll? What about a Beanie Baby? What about an action figure?

Perhaps the most famous, loved, and timeless stuffed animal is the teddy bear. It is widely believed to be a source of comfort to children. A stuffed bear or other plush animal is often the first gift given to a new baby. It is not at all uncommon for very young children (and some not-so-young children) to carry their stuffed animals with them everywhere and to become very upset if they are separated from them.

## Teddy Bears

At least in the United States, this infatuation with teddy bears dates back to the early 1900s. The name "Teddy" bear originated from a hunting incident in 1902 that involved then President Theodore Roosevelt. Roosevelt refused to shoot an exhausted black bear that had been chased by hounds. The incident inspired a cartoon, which, in turn, inspired a toy maker to create a new toy that he called a teddy bear. As soon as it arrived in the stores, it was a smash hit here and abroad. By 1903 the teddy bear craze was so widespread that everyone jumped on the bandwagon—children, grown women, and even Roosevelt, who used one as a mascot in his bid for reelection in 1904.

In 2006, more than 100 years since its introduction to the toy market, retail sales of stuffed plush animals—including teddy bears—were $1.3 billion. In these past 100 years, other stuffed animals, for example, Barney and Elmo, have captured the hearts of children—boys and girls alike. One change reflective of the pervasive boys-and-girls-are-so-different theme: Gund and other toy manufacturers are now making blue teddy bears!

On Amazon, the best-selling toy for Christmas of 2009 was Mr. Squiggles, a stuffed hamster. The ads for him proclaimed: "He is equipped with technology to enable him to talk and scurry around your home just like a real creature. And he loves to be cuddled!"[8] Both boys and girls love these warm, cuddly toys, call them what you will.

## For Kids, It's Paws, Not Jaws

As children grow older, real pets often add to or replace stuffed animals in children's affections. As parents, we all know how thrilled children are to have a pet. Depending on what kind of pet a child has, she or he wants to hold it, play with it, kiss it, and sleep with it. Of course, not all girls want pets, nor do all boys. Neither do all girls and boys take equally to caring for their pets. But most children, boys and girls, are equally attached to and eager to care for their animal friends.

In a series of studies, psychologists Gail Melson, of Purdue, and Alan Fogel, of the University of Utah,[9] looked at how nurturance *develops* during childhood. They found that before the age of 4 or 5, boys and girls are equally caring toward both younger children and the elderly. Their findings dovetail with a major international study of 12 different cultures[10] that found boys of all ages to be quite responsive to infants and toddlers. Boys are assigned child-care duties far less often than their sisters are, but in every culture they were observed to treat babies and toddlers in an overwhelmingly positive, friendly, and nurturant way.

However, among children 5 and older, gender differences appear. Specifically, boys and girls begin to describe caring for babies, for example, as "a mommy thing," and young girls by age 5 are more likely to respond with nurturing behaviors toward a baby (or assist a mother who requests help with such care).

Fascinatingly, however, "when nurturance is directed at animals (one's own or other people's pets), there are no gender differences in attitudes, motivations or behavior."[11] It appears that among preschool and older children, nurturance varies depending on the context.

Some "targets" of care are defined as "gender appropriate"—like dolls for girls—and others as "gender neutral," okay for both boys and girls. In particular, caring for animals is perceived by children as gender neutral.[12] Boys and girls are equally capable of nurturing behavior, although the target of their caring changes over time, most likely due to gender stereotypes.

Caring for pets is a gender-neutral activity even among adults. Those who argue that males are incapable of nurture need only to watch boys and grown men interact with their pets. Remember the well-loved TV series *Lassie*? It was one of the longest-lived dramatic series on television, running from 1954 to 1973. Initially, Lassie was the constant companion of fictional 11-year-old Jeff Miller, who lived with his mother and his grandfather in a small farming community. Later, 7-year-old Timmy Martin and his adoptive parents took over as Lassie's caretakers. Anyone who has watched this series knows that these two boys were as nurturant and loving to Lassie as one can imagine. No signs here of any repressed male-caring instincts.

On a practical note, according to Melson, about 75 percent of all U.S. children will grow up with pets in the home (similar estimates for Western Europe), "while shrinking family size and institutional care of the elderly means that children (both boys and girls) are less and less likely to learn about and experience nurturance of dependent humans within the home." Boys have as great a capacity for nurturing as girls, but thanks to the straitjacket of stereotypes, they are less likely to have had hands-on experience caring for younger siblings or babysitting, and are likely to exhibit nurturance only in certain situations.

As it turns out, parents play a major role in boys' nurturing behavior. Psychologist Judith Blakemore,[13] from Indiana University–Purdue University, Fort Wayne, found no difference in the amount of praise mothers bestow on sons and daughters for lovingly attending to baby siblings. However, children from more traditional homes—those whose parents subscribe to more-stereotypical gender roles—show a greater sex difference in nurturing behavior than children from more-egalitarian homes. Four-year-old boys with more-egalitarian parents were virtually indistinguishable from girls of the same age in the amount of interest they demonstrated toward babies. So this research suggests that parents' actions (role modeling) speak louder than their words (praise or disapproval) in shaping children's nurturing behavior.[14]

## *Sesame Street*'s Muppets

Fortunately for parents, popular culture offers young children many good images of caring males—unlike material designed for teenagers, which is all too often dominated by images of male violence and mayhem. It is striking that so many of the cartoon, comic strip, and TV children's show characters targeting young audiences are so counterstereotypical. Charlie Brown is a loser, Lucy is selfish and mean, and Lassie's caretakers are loving boys.

One of the most influential and long-lasting children's TV programs is *Sesame Street*. What do the *Sesame Street* Muppets tell us about boys and girls and caring? Although most of the Muppets are male characters (Ernie, Bert, Big Bird, Elmo, Cookie Monster, Kermit the Frog, Oscar the Grouch, Grover, Mr. Snuffleupagus), they are patient, caring, and certainly non-aggressive. They know how to relate to one another and are sensitive to each other's needs. The few female characters (Zoe, Rosita, and the newest addition, Abby Cadabby) are also atypical. Zoe is Elmo's tomboy friend, Rosita is an emerald blue bilingual Muppet, and Abby is a 3-year-old fairyin-training. Her designer explains that Abby was introduced to help combat the "mean-girl syndrome." However, she is no wannabe Tinkerbell. Even though she has long lashes, frilly costumes, and enjoys dressing up, she's smart, funny, and she has a great desire to learn everything. (The other female character, Miss Piggy, makes occasional appearances on the show but is not part of the regular cast.)

## Male Models on Children's TV

*Wiggles* is a group of four men in their late twenties that has become an international sensation. They have created a catalog of music, television, video, and film that has enchanted young children all over the world. They write their own music and lyrics and have won countless awards for their albums. They are upbeat, optimistic, and clearly caring guys.

*Mister Rogers' Neighborhood*, a children's television series that was created and hosted by Fred Rogers, is the second-longest-running series on PBS, after *Sesame Street*. The series could be seen in reruns on most PBS stations until September 1, 2008, when it was removed by PBS from its daily syndicated schedule.

*Mister Rogers' Neighborhood* was characterized by its quiet simplicity and gentleness. Episodes did not have a plot; they consisted of Rogers speaking directly to the viewer about various issues, taking the viewer on tours of factories, demonstrating experiments, crafts, and music, and interacting with his friends. The half-hour episodes were punctuated by a puppet segment chronicling occurrences in the Neighborhood of Make-Believe.

At the beginning of each episode, Fred Rogers enters his television studio house, singing "Won't You Be My Neighbor?" He hangs his coat in a closet, puts on a cardigan zipper sweater, and removes his dress shoes to put on sneakers. One of Mr. Rogers' sweaters now hangs in the Smithsonian Institution, a testament to the cultural influence of his simple daily ritual.

Rogers covered a broad range of topics over the years, and the series did not gloss over issues that other children's programming avoided. In fact, Rogers endeared himself to many when, on March 23, 1970, he dealt with the death of one of his pet goldfish. The series also dealt with competition, divorce, and war. Rogers returned to the topic of anger regularly and focused on peaceful ways of dealing with angry feelings.

When Fred Rogers died in 2003, the PBS website communicated some ways to help children deal with Mr. Rogers' death by presenting suggestions to parents of what to say to the children about Mr. Rogers and how to approach a child who inquired about him.

Though *Mister Rogers' Neighborhood* no longer runs regularly on PBS, individual member stations have the option of airing the *Neighborhood* independently of the PBS syndicated feed. WQED, in particular, is continuing to air the series daily, and there is currently a campaign to urge PBS and all member stations to bring the show back five days a week.

## Girls, Boys, and Empathy

Fred Rogers, the Muppets, and many other characters designed for young children spend a lot of time in situations dealing with empathy—how we should feel and behave toward other people. Why is it important to teach children about empathy? That's the critical question that Lise Eliot asks. Her answer? Because without it, our society fractures into individual atoms and can't hold together. And, as she notes, boys can learn to be empathetic if parents and teachers don't fall into the trap of thinking that such behavior isn't "normal" for them. As we saw in chapter 3, boys' brains don't hamper their ability to nurture.

Whether or not we are all "hardwired" for nurturing and empathy, it's clear that we fire up such emotions by our actions. Giving or receiving, we learn how to better relate to one another.

In fact, boys have to *learn* to suppress emotions, and too often our culture instructs them well. Harvard psychiatrist William Pollack,[15] the author of *Real Boys*, notes that our strict "boy culture" demands emotional rigidity, and by second grade erodes the "interpersonal" skills that come naturally to boys. He says that boy babies are actually *more* expressive and vocal than girl babies. "We now have executives paying $10,000 a week to learn emotional intelligence. These [sessions] actually target skills boys were born with."

In fact, girls and women may have no natural advantage over boys and men when it comes to empathy. Psychologist Faye Crosby, of the University of California, Santa Cruz,[16] methodically examined all of the scientifically well-designed studies comparing males and females with regard to empathy, altruism, cooperativeness, nurturance, and intimacy and found "no conclusive evidence to show that men and women differ from one another in the extent to which they attend to and are good at interpersonal relationships." It's clear, says Crosby, that many factors affect how you relate to other people—your social class, age, religion, nationality, education, personality, and especially the situation you're in at the moment. Your sex is only one variable, and not necessarily the most important one. As we've seen in earlier chapters, situation, not sex, is often more important.

Crosby also designed a series of questions to investigate women's "relational" qualities. She asked both male and female undergraduates: Is your self-concept wrapped up in social interactions? Do you need and enjoy the company of others? Do you learn in social situations better than in impersonal or mechanical situations? Are you swayed in your opinions and attitudes by others?

Crosby indeed found that females' self-concept depends on social approval—but the same is true for males. Females enjoy being in the company of others—just as much as males do. Social factors such as teachers' or supervisors' approval are important for women—and just as important for men. And females are not easier to persuade than men. "Under some circumstances, everyone acts like a spineless jellyfish; and under other circumstances, everyone shows strength and independence."

In laboratory studies, men respond even more intensely than women to strong emotional stimuli. The catch is that their responses are mostly internal. Compared to women, men undergo greater increases in heart rate, blood pressure, and sweating when confronted with highly emotional situations. So, even though men's emotions are less visible on the surface, they are just as powerful as women's.

Because of these different (learned) ways of expressing nurturant feelings, men seem less emotional and more detached than women. You have to probe beneath the surface behavior to discover what is actually going on. When you do, there is ample evidence that the observed gender differences are not innate but rather are shaped and reinforced by powerful social mores.

This social indoctrination begins in childhood and has a lasting effect. Boys who can express their feelings stand a better chance of understanding feelings in other people. Such fortunate boys are more likely to develop meaningful and effective communication with their future spouses, with their coworkers, and eventually with their own children.

In *Men Are from Mars and Women Are from Venus*, John Gray[17] argues that men must naturally retreat to their "caves" in the face of situations that create emotional tension. But if boys are allowed to express their feelings and talk about them openly, when they grow up they may not have to flee to dark, lonely places when their wives or children confront them with emotional issues.


Fathers

Today, the men that boys grow up to be are often a far cry from the distant dads of 1950s lore or the repressed, career-fixated hollow men of Nancy Chodorow's scenario. Men, in fact, can parent as well as women can, and often do.

Sociologist Barbara Risman,[18] from the University of Illinois at Chicago, found that fathers who had primary responsibility for child care were just as nurturant as mothers were. Louise Silverstein and Carl Auerbach,[19] psychologists at Yeshiva University, found similar results. They looked at major studies involving men from 10 different subcultures in the United States and reported that fathers can be just as good at parenting as mothers. Children can thrive with males doing most or all of the parenting. Data from studies of two-parent families in which the father is the primary caretaker, single fathers, and families headed by gay fathers tell a consistent story: There is nothing unnatural about fathering, and men are not simply inadequate substitutes for mothers.

Researchers find no evidence that men, by their nature, can't nurture infants and children. Cross-cultural evidence shows that there is no "natural" kind of fathering behavior. Fathers can be distant and barely involved with children, or they can be highly involved. According to Silverstein and Auerbach, the idea that men lack a biological basis for nurturing just doesn't jibe with the research: "The neo-conservative position is simply wrong about men not having a natural inclination to parent." David Blankenhorn's idea that men should just be "pals" to their children has no basis in science.

The trend toward fathers getting more involved with their kids and knowing them better is clear and well documented. Data from the National Study of the Changing Workforce[20] show that for the first time, fathers are spending more time with their children than on their own personal interests and pursuits. An analysis of national data just released from the Institute for Social Research[21] at the University of Michigan reports that fathers significantly increased their time with children (from 19 to 23 hours a week) between 1981 and 1997. Our major study of dual-earner couples found that when kids reach school age, fathers spend as much time in child care as do mothers. The Changing Workforce study finds the same trend.

Attitudes are changing as well as behavior. Studies of men of all ages, from high school up, show an increasing trend toward endorsing more-liberal views of men's and women's gender roles. Once, research found, many men didn't talk about the child care they did for fear of being ridiculed. Now, only a minority of men thinks it's appropriate for men to be sole breadwinners while women stay home to do all the child care. Younger men, it seems, are focused on fatherhood more than men were in the past. A national survey by the Radcliffe Public Policy Center, released in 2000,[22] found that men between the ages of 20 and 39 were more likely to give family matters top billing over career success. Eighty-two percent put family first, and 71 percent said they would sacrifice part of their pay to have more time with their families. These findings are consistent with the results of surveys at such major corporations as DuPont and Merck.

Although today we hear a lot about "absent fathers," when fathers are on the scene, as they often are, they are very involved in their children's lives. John Snarey, of Emory University,[23] reviewed a major, four-decades-long study of fathers and sons and concluded that the traditional image of Dad as the shadowy figure in the background while Mom does all the nurturing is erroneous. Snary says that old—and widely quoted—studies showing that fathers spend few hours each week with their children and "help out" as parents are passé. "These findings are historically dated and culturally limited," he says. U.S. census data indicate that fathers now provide 25 percent of primary child care for preschool-age children; in two-earner families, fathers take sole responsibility for child care at double the rate of men in single-earner families.

Data from the 2008 National Study of the Changing Workforce[24] document Dad's parenting. Employed fathers, especially Millennials (those born between the late 1970s and mid-1990s) are spending more time with children today than their age counterparts did three decades ago, whereas employed mothers' time spent with children has not changed significantly. On average, employed fathers of all ages spend 3.0 hours per workday with children under 13, compared with 2.0 hours in 1977. For employed mothers of all ages, average time spent with children has remained at 3.8 hours. Today's Millennial fathers spend 4.3 hours per workday compared with the 2.4 hours spent by their age counterparts in 1977. Mothers under 29 years of age today spend, on average, 5.0 hours with their children, compared with 4.5 hours in 1977. Overall, today's men are taking increasing responsibility for the care of their children. In 1992, 21 percent of women said that their spouses or partners were taking as much or more responsibility for the care of their children as they were. By 2008, that percentage had risen to 31 percent. Interestingly, 49 percent of men reported taking as much or more responsibility for the children as their wives, indicating a perception gap.

It's clear that the capacity to nurture exists in all of us, male and female. How it develops has more to do with how we raise and educate our children, and with the messages society sends us than with any inborn gender-related caring "instincts."

# 9 THE IDEAL CLASSROOM

There's a new vision of the ideal classroom—one for girls, and one for boys.

The girls' classroom is filled with quiet, focused girls who are comfortable sitting at their desks for long periods of time. The teacher speaks to them in hushed tones, and classical music may be playing in the background. The girls learn about subjects such as chemistry by analyzing "girly" artifacts like cosmetics or perfume or cleaning fluids.

In the boys' classroom there's a lot of noise and activity, as the boys move about, expend a lot of physical energy, and work on hands-on projects such as taking a motorcycle apart to understand the principle of how engines work.

More and more classrooms across American are being set up according to this model.

In 2009, the *Today* show[1] profiled a single-sex school located in suburban St. Louis. The segment began with a video showing boys engaging in calisthenics and girls sitting quietly at their desks reading and writing. Boys were permitted to learn anywhere in the classroom:

under their desks, in tents, or standing on chairs. No similar alternative learning opportunities were provided for girls. And the reading materials for the two genders were quite different. Boys read stories featuring monsters while girls read stories featuring movie stars. Yet when the school administrator was interviewed, she insisted that the school avoided stereotyping in the classroom. In South Carolina, teachers do indeed teach girls chemistry by analyzing cosmetics.[2] And the state has just set the goal of having sex-segregated classrooms available to every child within five years. About 70 schools offer segregated classes now, and the goal is to have programs available to every child within five years.

Meanwhile, in a middle school in Mobile County, Alabama:

- Only girls were offered a drama class.
- While there were four different boys' computer applications classes, there was no computer applications class for girls.
- From a November 24, 2008, *Mobile Press Register* article: "Pencils in hand, the sixth-grade girls were encouraged to use as many descriptive words as possible as they wrote about their dream wedding cake. Would you like chocolate or vanilla? What colors should the icing be? Is 30 inches too big for the bottom tier?"

Down the hall, the boys in another sixth-grade class were asked one by one to give examples of action verbs used in sports. "Throw. Sack. Slam. Intercept. Applaud."

In another Alabama middle school,[3] teachers are encouraged to gear examples to a gender when possible. An example of a writing prompt for a boy may be what place in the world he would most like to go hunting or to drive on a racetrack, while girls may write about their dream wedding dress or their perfect birthday party. This ideal classroom—classrooms, actually, separated by gender—could wind up being harmful to both boys and girls. The creation of these classrooms is being pushed hard by activists with an agenda, who present a great deal of questionable science about how boys and girls differ.

Teachers and administrators too often fall hard for this narrative, because on the surface it looks so authoritative, larded with scientific studies and few qualifications. And it holds out the promise of improving students' performance without the expenditure of large and all too often unavailable financial resources that are needed to provide first-class teaching materials and decent salaries for recruiting excellent teachers.

For example, Leonard Sax, best-selling author and executive director of the National Association for Single Sex Public Education, claims that girls hear 10 times better than boys. He writes, "Anytime you have a teacher of one sex teaching children of the opposite sex, there's a potential for a mismatch, if only in decibel level." He adds, "If a male teacher speaks in a tone of voice that seems normal to him, a girl in the front row may feel that he is yelling at her." He claims that boys do best in school when they are yelled at by female teachers. He goes on to claim that these "built-in" gender differences in hearing have a real impact, governing how parents should talk to their children and how classrooms should be organized.[4]

Michael Gurian,[5] best-selling author of *The Wonder of Boys* and a strong advocate of teaching boys and girls very differently, chimes in as well: "Because girls and women are able to hear things better than boys and men, sometimes a loud voice is needed for boys. This fact makes an interesting basis for keeping boys near the front of the physical classroom."

This idea is often repeated in the media, in parenting columns, and in the blogosphere. In a 2009 *Seattle Times* story,[6] the reporter writes, uncritically, "In a classroom, male brains zone out easily unless teachers know how to keep them glowing. Boys need to move around; the teacher needs to be louder and more animated, for a start. "

But is there any real science behind this notion? Not really.

Sax bases his argument that girls hear better than boys on two papers published in 1959 and 1963 by psychologist John Corso. Mark Liberman,[7] a linguistics professor at the University of

Pennsylvania, has become something of a scientific gumshoe by tracking down specious gender-differences arguments. We've cited some of his work earlier. Sax is one of his favorite targets, and he has spent a fair amount of energy examining the original research behind Sax's claims.

In Corso's 1959 study, for example, the researcher didn't look at children; he looked at adults. You simply can't make classroom rules for kids from a study done only on adults. Sax uses several other hearing studies to make his case that a teacher who is audible to boys will sound too loud to girls. But Liberman says Sax misrepresents one study of the hearing levels of infants, reporting the *opposite* of what the researchers actually said. Here, he asserts, Sax moves from "carelessness to misrepresentation."

Overall, Liberman says, "if you really look at this research, it shows that girls' and boys' hearing is much more similar than different. What's more, the sample sizes in those studies [the ones Sax used]—are far too small to make meaningful conclusions about gender differences in the classroom."

The truth is that the tiny and insignificant differences between girls' and boys' hearing have no educational significance whatsoever! All those teachers who are yelling at boys and speaking softly to girls are doing so for no scientifically sound reason. "Dr. Sax isn't summarizing scientific research; he's making a political argument," says Liberman. "The political conclusion comes first, and the scientific evidence—often unrepresentative or misrepresented—is selected to support it."[8]

## The Eyes Have It

Much the same misrepresentations of the scientific data occur in Sax's and Gurian's pronouncements about gender differences in vision. They both repeatedly make much of the supposed fact that girls and boys see very differently. Gurian[9] claims, "New studies are indicating that even the cells in our retina may well be different."

An Education Week[10] blog picks up this idea: "Studies suggest that male retinas are better at detecting motion, while female retinas are better at seeing color and texture. As a result, girls tend to draw flowers and butterflies using bright colors, while boys draw cars and spaceships using drabber hues."

If the sexes indeed see very differently, the structure of the eye must be very different for each sex, and this variation must occur at a very early age. Not so, scientists say.[11]

To a remarkable degree, the eyes of *all* vertebrates are similar in structure and function; so similar as to be not much more than variations on the same theme. The size, shape, and function of the eye are dictated by the laws of optics and the wave length of the spectra to which it must respond. There aren't too many ways to do this; hence, a successful "design" that appeared early in the phylogeny of the vertebrates had been highly conserved throughout the entire line of vertebrate evolution, with appropriate species differences arising as modifications to the basic pattern.[12] (emphasis added)

With this background, how is it possible to justify claims that the visual systems of newborn boys and girls are vastly different—different enough to affect performance and to require separate learning environments?

Let's look at the claim that the retinas of boys and girls are so dissimilar that there is no overlap at all, as Leonard Sax purports.[13] To begin with, remember that the human embryo is not sex-differentiated structurally until about 6 weeks of age. If the retinas of boys and girls are dramatically different, then the development of the retina must begin after this initial unisex stage. However, evidence indicates that the process of embryonic eye development begins at about 22 days![14]

Early in embryonic development, the lens of the eye begins to differentiate. In these early days, the light-sensitive elements of the retina develop, as do the color-sensitive elements. Moreover, the cornea and the eyelids also become differentiated. At 41 days of age, the embryo has developed the major structural components of the retina (i.e., iris, cornea, pigment layer, and light-sensitive layer). Figure 9.1 shows a cross-section of the eye of a 41-day-old human embryo. Remember, the embryo is still not sex-differentiated.

With this developmental trajectory, how is it possible to justify claims that the visual systems of newborn boys and girls are vastly different—different enough to affect performance and to require separate learning environments?

Given this evidence, it is very unlikely that some interior mechanism of the eye makes girls draw colorful butterflies and boys draw drab rocket ships. There's an easier explanation at hand—just stroll up and down the aisles of your local toy store. All the girls' toys are in bright pinks and purples. All the boys' toys are in blues, blacks, and browns, or some variant thereof. We know that young kids are responsive to the gendered cues incorporated by marketers.

Remember the experiment we outlined in chapter 6 in which 5-year-olds identified the purple sparkly gun as a toy for girls and the dark spiky teapot as one for boys? There's no mystery in why kids draw in the colors that they do.

Another hallmark of the new "ideal" classroom—for boys—is a space where they can move around, hop in and out of their desks, maybe even stretch out on the floor while working on a project. Movement stimulates male brains and helps manage impulse behavior, claims Michael Gurian.[15] He even advocates that boys stand up while in class! Girls, on the other hand, he says, do not need to move around as much while learning.

Gurian has it exactly half right. He claims that boys' learning style requires more physical engagement. But guess what? Exercise accelerates the learning ability of girls just as much as it does that of boys.

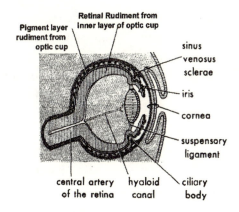

FIGURE 9.1    Cross-section of the Eye of a 41-day-old Human Embryo
*Source*: Adapted from D. T. Caceci, "Anatomy and Physiology of the Eye."

Professor Charles Hillman[16] and his colleagues at the University of Illinois at Urbana-Champaign agree that physical exercise has a significantly positive influence on academic performance. Hillman is a professor of kinesiology and community health and the director of the Neurocognitive Kinesiology Laboratory.

Data from a series of recent studies from his lab indicate that aerobic fitness is related to better performance on school-based achievement tests of mathematics and reading. Specifically, the data suggest that physical activity may increase students' cognitive control—or ability to filter out extraneous noise (i.e., distractions) and pay closer attention to the critical cues and act upon them.

In one study, the participants were 9-year-olds (8 girls, 12 boys). When the children performed the tasks after a burst of physical activity, their performance improved dramatically, compared to that of the control group that did not engage in physical exercise. How much improvement was there in actual classroom learning? To answer that question, the researchers gave the 9-year-olds an academic achievement test that measured performance in reading, spelling, and math. The kids got better scores following exercise. The biggest gain was in reading comprehension. In fact, according to Hillman, "If you go by the guidelines set forth by the Wide Range Achievement Test, the increase in reading comprehension following exercise equated to *approximately a full grade level* [emphasis added]. Thus, the exercise effect on achievement is not [just] statistically significant, but a meaningful difference."[17]

As we noted, girls' cognitive performance benefits from physical activity as much as boys' does. When Roz Barnett asked Professor Hillman if he found any gender differences in his studies, he replied, "No. We have never found sex differences in our work. We have included sex as a variable to investigate this question and never found support for it. I am unaware of any articles examining sex as a moderator of the exercise/cognition relationship."[18]

Lise Eliot agrees: "Everyone wins from creating a more developmentally appropriate classroom that fits the needs off *all* [young children]":

More movement

Less lecturing, more action

Training in inhibitory control

More manipulatives

Tempt them with technology

Practicing penmanship without penalty

Competition as a lure

Male teachers

The underlying brain mechanisms that are positively affected by exercise are the same for boys and girls. This fact is another nail in the coffin of the idea that major gender differences in brains affect academic performance and require that boys and girls be taught in different learning environments.

Despite these published facts, those who advocate separate classrooms speak as if the science had been settled—in their favor. David

Chadwell,[19] in South Carolina, is the country's first and only state-wide coordinator of single-sex education. Like Sax, he says that differences in eyesight, hearing, and the nervous system all should influence how you instruct boys. "You need to engage boys' energy, use it, rather than trying to say, *No, no, no.* So instead of having boys raise their hands, you're going to have boys literally stand up. You're going to do physical representation of number lines. Relay races. Ball tosses during discussion." For the girls, Chadwell prescribes a focus on "the connections girls have (a) with the content, (b) with each other and (c) with the teacher. If you try to stop girls from talking to one another, that's not successful. So you do a lot of meeting in circles, where every girl can share something from her own life that relates to the content in class."

## *CSI* in the Classroom?

This sort of "girly" classroom, in which teachers use cosmetics, jewelry, and references to cooking and friendships, is routinely touted by gender-difference advocates like Chadwell. But it may, in fact, not be what girls really want at all. Sugar and spice and everything nice is about as far away as you can get from a high school classroom described in the *New York Times* in a story headlined "A Hit in School, Maggots and All":[20]

> It's a sight that might make your skin crawl—if the chicken weren't already doing it for you.
>
> Projected onto the classroom screen was live-action footage of putrefying poultry, the image blown up to festively pulsating proportions by way of a digital microscope. And lively the action was: maggots of all ages and body-mass indexes wriggled across the slick carnal landscape, some newly hatched and ravenous, other older ones on the verge of pupating, looking as plump and pompous as earthworms.

But did the students in Scott Rubins' advanced forensic science class at New Rochelle High School shriek or go "Ewww gross" or even so much as wrinkle their noses with revulsion? Not over their dead bodies. For one thing, Mr. Rubins doesn't tolerate squeamish outbursts in the classroom. "No one is allowed to react," he said. "If you're reacting, you won't be able to learn."

For another, the students were too busy furiously waving their hands in the air, begging to be chosen as the day's evidence collectors. Far from being disgusted by the maggot-cam feed, they were desperate for the chance to snap on a pair of disposable rubber gloves and retrieve the rest of the decomposing chicken that Mr. Rubins had deposited outside a few days earlier. They wanted to pick up the slimy three-and-a-half-pound ex-bird and flip it this way and that, to lift the wings and the legs and find the dark, warm crevices where flies in training like to hide.

You'd never find this course earmarked for girls in a school system that advocates kind, gentle, more feminine atmospheres for girls.

But guess what? The girls loved it. According to Scott Rubins,[21] "girls make up easily 80 percent of the students in my forensic science classes." So much for the belief that in mixed-sex classes, girls will shy away from science, especially when it has to do with messy topics like decay and maggots.

The fact is that we should be worrying about—not celebrating—those classrooms in which girls sit still, huddle close together, and listen to soothing classical music.

If educators follow the prescription to encourage boys—but discourage girls—from physical activity while learning, good science tells us that girls will suffer. When ideology trumps science, poor educational policy results. Obviously, we should be working on giving both girls and boys more opportunity to exercise while they learn, not just focusing on boys.

Commenting on his own study of exercise and learning, Hillman says, "What we found in this particular study is, following acute bouts of walking, children's brain activity suggested that they are better able to allocate attentional resources." This effect is greater in more difficult conditions, the researchers say, "suggesting that when the environment is more noisy— visual noise in this case—kids are better able to gate out that noise and selectively attend to the correct stimulus and act upon it."[22] Given the preliminary study's positive outcomes, coauthor Darla Castelli[23] believes that these early findings could inform useful curricular changes. "Modifications are very easy to integrate," Castillo said. For example, she recommends that schools make outside playground facilities accessible before and after school.

"If this is not feasible because of safety issues, then a school-wide assembly containing a brief bout of physical activity is a possible way to begin each day," she said. "Some schools are using the Intranet or internal TV channels to broadcast physical activity sessions that can be completed in each classroom."

Other recommendations include scheduling outdoor recess as a part of each school day; offering formal physical education 150 minutes per week at the elementary level and 225 minutes at the secondary level; and encouraging classroom teachers to integrate physical activity into learning.

An example of how physical movement could be introduced into an actual lesson would be "when reading poetry (about nature or the change of seasons), students could act like falling leaves," she said.

In the new "ideal" classroom, which features separating girls and boys, teachers would also extend this segregation outside the classroom. They would assume that's it's "natural" for boys and girls to play separately. But in fact, do the boy-girl patterns of play we see in schoolyards today reflect styles that date back to prehistory? Probably not, anthropologists say. Our hunter-gatherer ancestors lived for eons in small nomadic groups. In all likelihood there were not many children in any one group, and the children were apt to be of different ages. (The sexes are more likely to separate from one another in same-age groups than they are in mixed-age groups.) So both sexes probably played freely with one another and the dominant "segregation" was between adults and children, not between boys and girls. We say that with some confidence because we see today that when children are in small groups, they play together without regard for sex. Moreover, in large extended families children tend to segregate by age, not by sex—the older kids (or big kids) versus the younger kids (or little kids).

It is also likely that the child's play of our genetic ancestors was not "gendered." Toys were probably few and created from sticks, stones, or any material that was available. Children played most often with whatever was around without a thought about whether it was a "girl thing" or a "boy thing." Our ancestors had no modern advertising to create pink and blue versions of the same toys to promote products for boys and girls.

So is sex-segregated play natural or created? Is what we often see in school really typical of children's natural behavior, or is it the result of being in a highly structured, rule-bound environment? Barrie Thorne,[24] a highly respected sociologist at the University of California, Berkeley, points out that what science knows about kids comes mainly from only one place: the schoolyard. That's not only the place where most segregation among children occurs; it's also the place where most developmental research on children takes place—90 percent, according to Thorne.

She approaches the study of childhood differently. She doesn't hone in on schoolyard behavior but follows kids all day, in many settings. Her work is extremely important because she collected her data by observing kids over long periods of time, and she is very sensitive to the context in which the children's behavior occurs. Thorne understands that kids' behavior varies over time and depends on what kind of school they are in, what kinds of teachers they have, and what activities they are engaged in. She doesn't fall into the trap of making generalizations about *all* kids at *all* times.

Thorne reports in her book *Gender Play* that sex segregation occurs only when there are large groups of same-age children who are supervised publicly by few adults. In other, more private and intimate settings, cross-sex play occurs often and easily. And these are the settings in which people spend most of their time—now and in the past.

Not until the rise of industrialization were children sent out of the home to school, where there were enough of them to permit sex segregation and where there were few adults charged with their supervision. When you have one or two teachers watching over many kids playing in a schoolyard, you have to find ways to organize them. Sex is the most the obvious category. But it's unlikely that gender was important in determining how kids played back in hunter-gatherer times (roughly 2,000,000–8,000 B.C.) in which children played in small groups of kin.

So the segregation we see among schoolchildren may itself be an adaptation to an "unnatural" set of circumstances for which we are genetically ill-prepared. Sex-segregated play may have been created by the institution that we devised to educate children in the most convenient way, *not* by the nature of children themselves. "At school, no one escapes being declared male or female whether that difference is relevant or not," Thorne says. What matters most in the schoolyard is the way in which children can be easily grouped (boys on the right, girls on the left). In families, on the other hand, what matters most to parents is the individual qualities of their children. In our culture, the model of sisters and brothers offers one of the few powerful images of relatively equal relationships between girls and boys and between adult men and women. The relationships between brothers and sisters begin in childhood, a period in which gender relations *in the family* are relatively egalitarian.

When young kids aren't in school, they don't display much sex segregation. In neighborhoods, you find a lot more mixing of the sexes than in school. In one neighborhood we know, girls and boys are in and out of each other's houses, they ride bikes together, roller-blade and shoot hoops together. If there *are* two cultures, they are so fluid that many kids move in and out of them with ease. Even in schools, boys and girls often interact in classrooms, school plays, orchestras, interest clubs, etc. And one study of how kids behave in a children's museum finds very little segregation between boys and girls.

Peas in a Pod?

The focus on difference between the sexes is so overdone that little attention is paid to "within-sex" difference. Boys often differ more from one another in their temperaments, their styles of play, and other such factors than they do from girls. And vice versa. Ask any parent who has two children of the same sex if they are carbon copies. More often than not, one boy will be outgoing and sports-minded while the other is more bookish, preferring to spend time alone and able to amuse himself for hours. Or one girl will be a rowdy tomboy while her sister loves dolls and dressing up. But too many experts ignore this reality and focus only on boy-girl differences. (Also, the situation makes a huge difference. When kids are roller-blading together, for example, their sex doesn't much matter. But when they are trying out for the gymnastics team or the football team, sex makes a big difference.)

When kids are being watched by adults, Thorne notes, boys and girls are more likely to avoid one another. Their behavior changes when the situation changes—when they're lining up on their own for the cafeteria, trying out for band, or playing spontaneously, boys and girls don't separate. At one elementary school Thorne studied, fifth grader Kevin arrived in the schoolyard with a ball. Seeing potential action, another boy, Tony, walked over "with interest on his face." Rita and Neera were already standing on the playground nearby. Neera called out, "Okay, me and Rita against you two" as Kevin and Tony moved into position. The handball game began in earnest with serves and returns punctuated by game-related talk—challenges between the opposing teams. ("You're out!" "No, exactly on the line.") and supportive comments between team members ("Sorry, Kevin," Tony said when he missed his shot. "That's okay," Kevin replied). The game went on for about five minutes—no evidence of sex segregation here. Then other children began to arrive. One more girl joined Rita and Neera, and three more boys joined Kevin and Tony. One was John, a dominant leader among the boys. Suddenly the game changed from a casual one in which boys and girls happened to be on different sides to a "highly charged sense of girls-against-the boys/boys-against-the-girls." Each sex started jeering and teasing the other. Finally boys and girls started chasing each other, and that broke up the game.

Why did John's arrival have such a big effect? The other boys didn't want him to see them as sissies, and he encouraged the jeering at the girls. If you happened on the field at that moment, you'd see a "snapshot" of highly segregated play. If you'd arrived a few minutes earlier, you'd have seen casual, relaxed mixed-sex play. John is a leader. He's dominant and assertive, and he draws attention to himself. He's exactly the kind of boy that researchers notice, and therein lies a major problem with the two-cultures model—*who* gets studied.

"The focus is usually on kids (like John) who behave the way we expect them to—the dominant boys and the passive girls," says Thorne. "Kids who don't fit the pattern get ignored." Most boys, for example, aren't "dominant" most of the time. If you have a hierarchy, you have to have a lot of subordinates. Thorne sees "a skew towards the most visible and dominant" which leads to a silencing and marginalization of the majority. She sees a "Big Man Bias" in research on children, which equates the behavior of male elites with "typical" boy behavior. "Other kinds of boys may be mentioned, but not as the core of the gender story." However, more than half of the boys in a classroom she examined intensively did *not* fit into the rigid stereotype of the way boys are supposed to behave.

But it's not only in research that this bias exists. Many of the popular new books written for parents about how boys get short-changed in school (including *The War Against Boys* by Christina Hoff Sommers[25] and *The Wonder of Boys*[26] by Michael Gurian) portray only one kind of boy. He's dominant, rough-and-tumble, assertive; he hates to sit still and is not very articulate. But many boys are not like that at all. They're not physically aggressive, not into sports, are highly verbal, love to read, and are able to converse at a high level with adults.

In one of the classrooms Thorne observed, she found four boys—Jeremy, Scott, Bill, and Don—whose relationships were exactly like the intimate, sharing modes of connecting that are usually ascribed to girls. "Jeremy, who had a creative imagination, spun fantasy worlds with one boy at a time . . . acting as detectives tracking footprints on the playground. Jeremy and his partner would share treasured objects." The identity of Jeremy's adventuring partner of the moment shifted between the boys via a "break-up" process often claimed to be typical of girls. "The boy on the outs would sometimes sulk and talk about the other two behind their backs." When Scott was excluded, he would activate a long-standing affiliation with Don. When Bill was on the outs, he went solo. "Over the course of the school year I saw each of the shifting pairs, Jeremy and Bill, Jeremy and Scott, Scott and Don—celebrate themselves as 'best buddies.'" The pattern of their relationships, Thorne says, "fit the shifting alliances claimed to typify girls' social relationships, but *boys* were the protagonists."

The behavior of these boys would be familiar to Niobe Way,[27] professor of applied psychology at New York University. She finds that the widely held notion that young teenage boys can't—or won't—express emotion is all wrong. Boys at this age can be "downright sentimental" about their friendships. When she asked about their best friends, boys often said, "They won't laugh at me when I talk about serious things." From her lengthy interviews, she found that teens defied the one-dimensional image of boys in popular culture. Yet, she says, "this notion of this emotionally illit-erate, sex-obsessed, sports-playing boy just keeps getting spit out again and again."

Are Learning Styles the Key?

"Are you a verbal learner or a visual learner?" asks *Science Daily*.[28] "Chances are, you've pegged yourself or your children as either one or the other and rely on study techniques that suit your individual learning needs. And you're not alone—for more than 30 years, the notion that teaching methods should match a student's particular learning style has exerted a powerful influence on education. The long-standing popularity of the learning styles movement has in turn created a thriving commercial market amongst researchers, educa-tors, and the general public."

Schools have spent millions of dollars, and parents and teachers have bought books and videos and designed curricula around the idea that if you can match these materials to a child's learning style, that child will flourish academically.

Unfortunately, there's no real basis for such claims, according to a major 2009 report[29] published in *Psychological Science in the Pub-lic Interest*. Despite the fact that numerous studies have purported to show the existence of different kinds of learners (such as "audi-tory learners" and "visual learners"), those studies have *not* used the type of rigorous research methods that would make their findings credible. No fewer than 71 different models of learning styles have been proposed over the years. Most have no doubt been designed with students' best interests in mind to create better environments for learning. But psychological research has not found that people learn differently, at least not in the ways learning-styles proponents claim. Given the lack of scientific evidence, the authors argue that the currently widespread use of learning-style tests and teaching tools is a wasteful allocation of limited educational resources. So, obviously, separating boys and girls on the basis of alleged learning-style differences is totally unscientific.


## The Real Ideal

There is an ideal classroom—and it's not one that shoehorns girls and boys into little pink and blue boxes. It's a classroom in which teachers see students as individuals and encourage them to stretch beyond stereotypes and discover a range of talents. The lens of gender—like those of race, class, or ethnicity—is not a helpful way to look at children.

What really works? Here's an example. As reported in the *New York Times* (April 26, 2010), P.S. 172, a 580-student primary school in an urban, high-poverty district in Brooklyn, is "among the city's top dozen schools." What is especially remarkable is that this is a school in which 80 percent of its students quality for free lunch, nearly a quarter of the students receive special education services, and many of its largely Hispanic population live in homes in which English is not spoken.

How well are the students at P.S. 172 doing academically? In 2009, for example, all 75 fourth graders passed the math assessment, with all but one student receiving a score of "advanced." In English, all but one of the fourth graders performed at or above grade level. Those results are more typical of suburban schools with more-advantaged student populations and higher per-capita school budgets.

Mr. Spatola, the principal, attributes the school's success to a comprehensive laser-beam approach. Each student's strengths and weaknesses are initially assessed by the classroom teacher, who develops an individualized instructional plan for each student. The plan is constantly reviewed and revised to accommodate the needs of the student. When a teacher notices that a student is not making the expected progress, the teacher reaches out to the supervisors and the academic coaches. The coaches and supervisors work with the teacher to evaluate the needs of the student and, if necessary, bring into the process the school's clinical speech pathologist, occupational therapist, and clinical psychologist. Together the team members develop a strategy for building on the student's academic strengths and addressing weaknesses. This individual approach has, according to Mr. Spatola, the best odds of overcoming obstacles to academic success. Moreover, it doesn't require breaking the bank. In fact, thanks to careful budgeting and prudent fiscal management, the school's per child costs are actually lower than the city's average.

We asked Mr. Spatola whether there were gender differences in achievement or in strategies among his pupils. His answer was no. He found no gender differences when he examined math, English, or science scores. He strongly disagrees that educational standards are too high or that they should be lowered for boys in English, as some argue. Nor does he think that the curriculum needs to be adjusted to be "boy friendly." In fact he rejects a one-size-fits-all approach to pedagogy. Rather, he insists that learning occurs maximally when teachers focus on individual students' interests and skills, not their gender.

The more children see themselves as part of a group, the more vulnerable they are to "stereotype threat," a concept we outlined in our math chapter. Remember, when children internalize the idea that the group they belong to is not good at some skill, they actually do worse on tests of that skill if they are reminded of that fact. When girls are told that girls in general aren't good at math, they perform worse than they do when told nothing at all about this notion.

Too often the classroom is a place where gender becomes an issue even though it actually has no relevance to the main job of teachers and kids: learning. It can start with the ordinary greeting of teachers to their class. "Good morning, boys and girls." Teachers would never say "Good morning, blacks and whites." Or "Good morning, Latinos and Asians." Sometimes teachers line kids up for spelling bees with girls on one side and boys on the other, or march kids to the lunchroom or to an assembly in all-boy or all-girl lines.

Such practices, says Rebecca S. Bigler, associate professor of psychology at the University of Texas at Austin,[30] "lead children to believe that teachers are *intentionally* signaling the existence of important differences between genders—even when they are not."

Kids get a message that teachers don't intend to send, says Bigler. They "are likely to believe the people in that group share meaningful and unseen characteristics. That, then, is how the seeds of stereotyping are planted."

# IO SINGLE-SEX EDUCATION, PROS AND CONS

U.S. public schools are failing their students.

Seventeen of the nation's 50 largest cities had high school graduation rates lower than 50 percent, with the lowest graduation rates reported in Detroit, Indianapolis, and Cleveland, according to a report released in 2008. The report,[1] issued by America's Promise Alliance, found that about half of the public school students in the nation's largest cities receive diplomas. Students in suburban public high schools were more likely to graduate than their counterparts in urban public high schools, the researchers said.

Nationally, about 70 percent of U.S. students graduate on time with a regular diploma, and about 1.2 million students drop out annually.

"When more than 1 million students a year drop out of high school, it's more than a problem, it's a catastrophe," said former secretary of state Colin Powell,[2] founding chair of the Alliance.

Specifically, black and Hispanic students do worse than white students, and students from under-resourced urban school districts do worse than children from affluent suburban well-resourced school districts. Girls do better than boys overall, but the gender difference is swamped by differences in performance by race and social class.

Scholars have written volumes on the problems with our public education system and what to do about them. The only consensus is that the challenge of upgrading our schools so that our children will be well educated and able to compete in the new technology economy is multifaceted and defies easy fixes. Dilapidated schools must be rebuilt, teachers must be better trained in the subjects they teach, and they must be better paid so that talented individuals will be attracted to teaching and will not leave education for better-paying jobs in the private sector. Resources need to be upgraded: Textbooks need to be current; computers and other high-tech learning aids must be made widely available. Teachers and parents must believe in and motivate their children to excel. And on and on. All these costly reforms are being called for at a time when schools are facing budgetary cutbacks requiring layoffs of teachers, elimination of enrichment programs, and even four-day school weeks.

While thoughtful people are tackling these complex problems, a small but vocal group of self-styled educational gurus is proposing a simple, cheap, and according to them, effective resolution. Their answer—single-sex public education! Ignoring the large achievement gaps in race and social class, these champions focus exclusively on the much smaller (and growing even smaller) gender gap. What could be simpler—separate the girls and boys and teach according to "their brains" and student performance will improve.

Single-Sex Versus Coed Private Schools

It sounds like a magic bullet. One masterstroke and all our problems are solved. Advocates point to the nation's single-sex private schools, which are often among the best, and draw attention to the kids who ace the SATs, win prestigious scholarships, and go off in droves to the Ivy League. These advocates suggest that the same thing could happen if we simply segregated public school classrooms by gender. They prescribe this as the pattern that public schools should follow.

But what do we know about the academic and social outcomes of the country's private single-sex and coed primary and secondary schools? What are the experiences of the children who attend these elite schools? After all, if this is the model for solving our education problems, we need to know a lot about the schools that operate according to that model.

These seemingly easy questions are actually difficult to answer. There are good private schools and not-so-good private schools; some of the good schools are single-sex schools and some are not. The issue is whether their rankings have anything to do with the schools' sex composition.

There are some major problems with the research in this area. First, often the schools (or the national associations that represent them) commission a survey of their alums. How well prepared were they for college? Did their experiences in high school help them take on leadership roles? Would they repeat the girls' school experience if they had it to do over again? And so forth. It should also be noted that most studies in this area are conducted and/or funded by organizations that have a vested interest in the study outcomes.

And since the participants are those among the alums who choose to respond to the survey, they may well be biased toward viewing their school experiences positively. Thus, it is hard to interpret the results of such surveys, which tend to find overwhelming support for single-sex education. In one survey of 64 schools in the National Coalition of Girls' Schools (NCGS),[3] 88 percent of the alums said they would repeat the girls' school experience if they had to do it over again (88 percent either *definitely* or *probably*), and the overwhelming majority (84 percent) would encourage their daughters to have the same experience. In addition, almost all respondents (93 percent) either *somewhat* or *strongly agreed* that girls' schools provide greater leadership opportunities than coed schools.

In one area—preparation for academic and social interactions—the female alums were less positive. Specifically, 37 percent of the respondents perceived themselves to be more prepared than graduates of coed schools, but an equal number felt less prepared for academic interactions with men. About a quarter indicated that they were equally prepared. Moreover, the alums felt least prepared for social interactions with men. The breakdown: 52 percent perceived themselves to be less prepared in this regard than their coed-school counterparts, 30 percent felt equally prepared, and about 20 percent said they were more prepared for such interactions.

Again, it's hard to figure what to make of these self-reports. Compounding the problem is sorting out what features of the schools were associated with the positive responses. Was it the plentiful resources and individualized attention these schools provide? Was it the investment (monetary and emotional) their parents had made in their children's education? Was it the motivation of their peers, the expectations of their teachers? Indeed, was it any of the attributes of the schools per se, or was it the girls themselves?

The NCGS suggests that this latter explanation is the case. In general, school characteristics (e.g., whether the girls received financial aid or not, whether the schools were Catholic or non-Catholic) "were less associated with the major outcomes studied than were alumnae characteristics. This suggests that outcomes associated with girls' schools may have more to do with the girls themselves than with which schools they attend."

## Public Single-Sex and Coed Schools

In the public school arena, larger-scale studies have been done that rely less on self-report data and are not so tainted by the interests of the study funders or directors. In 2005, the Department of Education completed such a study.[4] An initial set of 2,221 studies was found to bear on this topic. Strikingly, after criteria of sound scientific research were applied, only 40 "met the inclusion criteria and were retained." In other words, only 2 percent of the published studies in this area were done with sufficient rigor to be included in the Department of Education's review!

A paltry crop, to be sure. The DOE's review included 32 outcomes (including all-subject achievement test scores, mathematics achievement test scores, science achievement test scores, grades, career aspirations, delinquency, post-secondary success, and so forth). With so many outcomes and so few studies (actually there were 112 findings in the 40 studies), it is not surprising that there were very few studies per outcome. Mathematics achievement test scores, English achievement test scores, and school subject preference were the only outcomes to have 10 or more qualifying studies.

Importantly, among the outcomes for which there were too few studies to draw any conclusions were post-secondary test scores, college graduation, graduate-school attendance, post-secondary unemployment, post-secondary success, choice of college major, opportunities for leadership roles in their high schools, satisfaction with their high school environment, and college satisfaction. These are precisely the areas in which single-sex education advocates claim their schools do better. But the evidence isn't there.

Other problems:

• The vast majority of the studies focused on secondary schools, making it impossible to develop any data-based evidence about the benefits or drawbacks of single-sex or coeducation in the primary grades.

• Most of the single-sex schools in the studies included in the DOE report were Catholic schools in which students are separated by sex only when entering adolescence. Therefore, opportunities to study single-sex elementary or middle schools in either the public or the private sector have been limited.

• There is no way to know whether results based on students in Catholic schools would generalize to students in non-Catholic schools. When parents decide to enroll a child in a Catholic school, they are also deciding to move the child out of the neighborhood school and are taking on financial costs. These decisions may reflect higher parental involvement and motivation on the part of parochial school students than public school students. It is clearly important, but difficult, to determine whether such selection factors have a large or small effect on the academic outcomes relative to public single-sex learning environments per se.

• Most studies focus on girls. Of the 40 studies that met the criteria for inclusion by the DOE, 20 focused exclusively on girls. When it came to academic outcomes, of those 20, 18 were split evenly between support for single-sex schooling and no differences (9 pro-single-sex and 9 no differences). The findings of the other studies were also mixed, showing no evidence that single-sex classrooms provide superior education.

• Too few researchers provide descriptive statistics on the students, or make available critical data such as effect sizes.

• Even within math, English, and school-subject preference, the three areas in which there were a reasonable number of studies, the studies differ in the criteria they use and in the statistical controls they employ in comparing single-sex and coed schooling. These limitations render it nearly impossible to draw any firm conclusions about the educational benefits of public single-sex or coeducation for girls or boys.

The data, in short, are a mess.


The California Single-Sex Public Education Experiment

While the published research data are ambiguous, a real-world experiment provides a clearer picture. One of the most ambitious experiments in single-sex education[5] took place in California in 1997. Governor Pete Wilson initiated a program with six schools, three for boys and three for girls. The intent of the program was to provide school choice, replicate the success of some private girls' schools, and offer urban boys positive role models. Students were drawn from the ranks of young people who needed the most help: those who had fallen behind in school, were experiencing trouble at home, or had already entered the correctional system.

All the single-sex schools closed within two years; only the San Francisco 49ers Academy in East Palo Alto, which enrolled girls and boys in two separate schools, is still open.

The State of California did not evaluate the schools and appropriated only $500,000 for their first two years of operation, expecting the schools thereafter to close or to become self-sufficient. Nevertheless, a three-year evaluation study was conducted from 1998 to 2000. More than 300 middle-school and high school students, educators, and parents were interviewed in six districts, each with separate girls' and boys' academies—12 schools in all, some on the same campus. The study[6] was conducted by Amanda Datnow, of the University of Toronto, with Lea Hubbard, of the University of California at San Diego, and Elisabeth Woody, of the University of California at Berkeley. The study, *Is Single Gender Schooling Viable in the Public Sector? Lessons From California's Pilot Project*, was funded by the Ford Foundation and the Spencer Foundation.

The study identified some benefits for both girls and boys: The single-sex setting in some cases eliminated social distractions and allowed for better concentration on academics and open discussion about dating and pregnancy. But according to the study's authors, these benefits were undermined because gender equity often was not addressed in the classrooms, gender stereotypes were often reinforced, and in some cases stereotypical behaviors were worsened.

"Single-gender, public academies need to guard against becoming a new form of tracking or resegregation," the report stated. "Segregation might lead to a safe or comfortable space for some populations, but they clearly create tensions for race and gender equity."

The academic success of both girls and boys was influenced more by small classes, strong curricula, dedicated teachers, and equitable teaching practices than by single-sex settings, the researchers said. These findings reinforced those of a 1998 study[7] by the American Association of University Women: Separating the sexes does not necessarily improve the quality of education for girls.

## Puffing Up Single Studies

Exacerbating the problem of ambiguous and hard-to-interpret data is the fact that the media often pick up findings from single studies and then exaggerate and distort them. For example, a 2009 article in the *Guardian*[8] had the following headline: "Girls Make Boys Worse at English, Says New Study." For his Ph.D., Steven Proud, the author of the study, tracked thousands of 7-, 11-, 14-, and 16-year-old boys' and girls' test results in English and math. His study was done in England between 2002 and 2004.

Proud,[9] a research student at Bristol University, concluded that boys should be taught English in single-sex classes, especially in the primary grades. In contrast, for both boys and girls, "a mix of the genders in both science and maths is optimal."

Let's take a closer look at just what Proud found. Boys did fractionally better in English when there were fewer girls in their classes, whereas girls' scores were unaffected. In addition, when it came to math and science, both boys and girls at primary school achieved up to a tenth of a grade more when there was a high proportion of girls in their classes.

But what does all this mean in real-life terms? To give you one example, the percentage of girls in a class would have to triple (i.e., go from 25 percent to 75 percent) for there to be a drop in boys' achievement by 0.075 standard deviations—a tiny change. In the other three cases—girls in English classes and boys and girls in math and science classes—either there was no difference as a result of the sex composition of the classes or both boys and girls showed marginal gains when there were more girls in the classroom.

Yet, according to Proud, his main point and the *only one given attention by the* Guardian, is that boys should be taught English in single-sex classes. You have to be a devotee of eeny-weeny differences to make such a bold prescription based on such minuscule data.

Professor Alan Smithers,[10] a leading researcher in single-sex education and director of the Centre for Education and Employment Research at the University of Buckingham, decried the hype. "This is one study, among many, which detects very small differences between boys and girls. But you can't say that it means boys or girls should be separated. It has very little practical importance for schools."

Nonetheless, the study received considerable media attention.

Interestingly, Proud also found that girls do better when there are some boys in their class who receive free school meals. Yet he does not conclude that girls should be taught in classes with more students who need meal subsidies. Clearly gender differences, no matter how small, are considered the "real story," more important than differences due to social class or perhaps other factors.

## The Good News About Coeducation

One of the arguments put forth by proponents of single-sex public education is that girls need to be in a same-sex environment so that they will be free to choose and excel in such "male" subjects as math.

Girls need to analyze cosmetics to understand chemistry, they need to be spoken to quietly, they need classrooms free of harsh questions and competition. In some of these arguments, girls seem like eggshells, easily breakable and too fragile for anything but delicate handling.

A lovely concept, but is it true? Not really. Remember the remarkable 2008 study funded by the National Science Foundation[11] that we reported on in our math chapter? These kids were mainly in public coed schools, and the researchers discovered that from every angle, girls measured up to boys. Even at the higher grades, when the students were taking harder courses, there were absolutely no meaningful differences in the math scores of boys and girls.

So, here are millions of girls, in regular classrooms, with no hand-holding, no classical music playing in the background, no cosmetics or household items in sight, and they are going great guns! Given the groundbreaking nature of the NSF study, the massive amount of data, the thoroughness of the analyses, and the remarkable findings, one might expect that the media would have jumped all over these counterintuitive results. Right?

Wrong. In a LexisNexis search of articles that appeared in major papers and journals in the year following the publication of this study, we found that the results were reported in only two major U.S. papers: the *New York Times* and the *Washington Post*. The *Times* ran a 1,300-word article in Section A; the *Post* ran a 123-word note. The rest of the world took more notice: there were two articles and an editorial in major Canadian papers, the *Irish Times* ran a story, as did the *Korea Times* and the *Sydney Morning Herald* in Australia. Other data[12] also suggest that girls in the UK and other Commonwealth countries are increasingly likely to take advanced science courses, as shown in figure 10.1.[13]

This increase is occurring at the same time that England, a country in which single-sex schools have been the norm, is moving very dramatically toward coeducation. At a minimum, the two trends shown in the figure suggest that girls' tendency to choose advanced math and science courses is not dependent on their attending single-sex schools.

In Canada, a major study of 18,000 students who attended coed or single-sex schools, some public, some private, found some important benefits for coeducation. Girls attending coed schools in Canada (both independent and public) felt more confident expressing

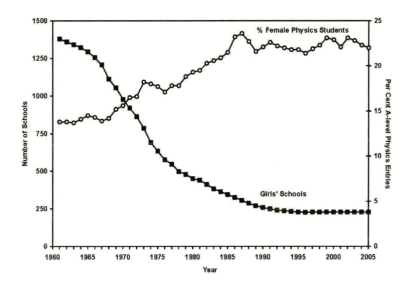

FIGURE 10.1    Girls' Schools and A-level Physics Entries
*Sources*: UK A-level physics entries from Smithers and Robinson (2006: chart 3.3).
Number of schools for England from annual volumes of *Statistics of Education:*
*Schools (DFE and DfES)*; up to 1977 schools data include Wales.

their views in the presence of male peers. And coed-school students were more likely than students in single-sex schools to agree that their peers respected members of the opposite sex.[14]

Clearly, the data presented thus far raise serious questions about two of the major reasons put forth by proponents of single-sex public education. The first is that cross-sex pressure makes it hard for girls to choose or excel in such "male" subjects as math and science. The impressive results just noted ought to put that argument to rest. The second is that boys' verbal abilities are thwarted because of the verbally drenched female curriculum in coed schools. Supposedly, this curriculum is biased against boys whose verbal abilities are limited. Once again, as we reported in chapter 4, solid data refute this argument.

## Studies from Other Countries

Most of the studies addressing the question of whether single-sex schools work come from other countries where single-sex education is often freely available. The results are mixed. The Australian Council for Education Research tracked 270,000 students over six years. The results indicated that boys and girls in single-sex classrooms scored an average of 15 to 22 percentage points higher than did boys and girls in coeducational settings. Graham Able,[15] of Dulwich College in London, found that children in single-sex education outperformed those in coeducational settings. In his research, widely published in British newspapers, boys seemed to benefit more than girls, challenging the traditional notions that it is the girls who get shortchanged in public school settings.

But other reports suggest that the single-sex programs don't really have any effect on student performance. Some argue that if these schools do show academic improvement, it's because they tend to attract young people who are driven and want to learn; scores therefore are bound to go up.

One major international review[16] of single-sex versus coed schools found that while there are some very good girls' schools and boys' schools, it does not look as though they are good *because* they are single-sex schools. The researchers found little evidence of consistent advantages for either single-sex education or coeducation.

In the United States, some states and cities have experimented with single-sex schools for disadvantaged kids. Some of these schools, like the Young Women's Leadership School of East Harlem, have produced impressive results. But from what we know from the research, the school's success probably is due not to the gender mix per se but to the pro-academic choice on the part of their parents/guardians as well as highly motivated teachers and excellent academic resources.

Overall Assessment

Given the seemingly small effects of separating or bringing the sexes together for education and the limitations on what educational research can and cannot do, it seems unlikely that evidence will ever be obtained that is sufficiently robust to cause the proponents of one approach or the other to change their views. This often seems to be the case in education, and in the social sciences generally. The paradox of single-sex education and coeducation is that the beliefs are so strong and the evidence is so weak.

To some readers, this chapter might be construed as an attack on single-sex education. That is absolutely not the case. One of us, Roz Barnett, attended only coeducational schools. The other, Caryl Rivers, went to a single-sex high school and college. We both got excellent educations. Our goal here has been to assess the quality of the evidence regarding educating the sexes together or separately. If we find ourselves looking harder at the claims for separating the sexes, it is because those lobbying for it have been so active in recent years.

Chief among the proponents is the U.S. National Association for Single Sex Public Education (NASSPE) and its president, Dr Leonard Sax. This is a group that takes great pains to look and sound scientifically impressive. If you took NASSPE at its word, you'd simply slam the book shut on the debate and declare, "Case closed."

The NASSPE website[17] lists nineteen studies that seem to make a very strong case for single-sex education. These include research attributed to Ofsted (Office for Standards in Education, Children's Services and Skills, UK), the Australian Council for Educational Research, and the National Foundation for Educational Research. In addition, the work of reputable academics and practitioners is featured on the website, along with Sax's own book *Why Gender Matters*.[18] The argument for sex segregation has been taken up by other websites as well, such as the National Coalition of Girls' Schools, is being repeated almost verbatim in academic papers,[19] and is trickling down through newspapers.[20] It is important, therefore, to examine in detail the evidence trumpeted by these websites. What you discover is that NASSPE seems to regard scientific studies like balloons—the more you puff them up, the more impressive they seem.

## NASSPE's Case

NASSPE's (2005) web page[21] titled "Single-Sex vs. Coed: The Evidence" begins by dismissing the U.S. Department of Education's study of single-sex education—the systematic review that we considered in detail above. The group calls the review "a disappointment" and "a missed opportunity." It also claims that "many studies [were] overlooked," which seems a bit rich, since so few studies were any good.

The lead evidence is taken from British researchers Mike Younger and Molly Warrington,[22] of the University of Cambridge. NASSPE says they found that single-sex classes are remarkably effective in boosting the performance of both girls and boys. But in fact, the researchers themselves were a lot more cautious.

In describing the results of their four-year study of more than 50 schools, they conclude that "as with other intervention strategies, however, there is the need for some caution in any analysis. Such single-sex classes are not a panacea in themselves." Although there were some positive effects for boys and girls "in some schools boys-only classes became very challenging to teach." Also, the "stereotyping of expectation established a macho regime which alienated some boys." And even in the most successful schools, both boys and girls said they did not want to be in single-sex classes for all lessons. Further, Younger and Warrington caution that for single-sex classes to work, a series of preconditions must be met: use of a proactive and assertive approach in the classroom; development of a team ethic; and strong involvement of senior administrators, staff, and parents—which is a tall order.

NASSPE also cites 18 other references that are grouped as (1) major nationwide studies, (2) "before and after studies," and (3) academic studies.

Of the cited studies, five are major nationwide studies. Ofsted is reported as demonstrating in 1998 that the superior performance of students in single-sex schools is *a direct result of single-sex education.* Quite authoritative, right? The only problem is that this striking finding has not been published by Ofsted, which has no knowledge of it.[23] Yet NASSPE references the finding in an article in the *Times Educational Supplement.*[24] This article reports a speech by Christine Agambar, then of Ofsted, to the annual conference in Oxford in 1998 of the Association of Maintained Girls' Schools. The only remark she makes about coed versus single-sex schools is to say that pupil eligibility for free school meals does not explain the difference in examination performance of single-sex and coeducational schools

This distortion of the data is classic NASSPE smoke and mirrors. Cite an impressive authority and assume that no one is going to check the source. When it turns out that the finding never existed and was attributed to a newspaper article that offers no relevant information, forget about it. Who's going to care?

Research from the Australian Council for Education Research has been similarly inflated. ACER's website carried a press release of a keynote address given by Australian researcher Kenneth Rowe to a conference in New South Wales in which he presented evidence of the better academic performance of girls and boys in a single-sex environment. But in his published accounts of the data, Rowe stresses that "it is important not to over-interpret the 'importance' of these gender and gender/class/school-grouping effects, since they pale into insignificance compared with class/teacher effects—regardless of student gender."

And, in a re-analysis eight years later, he and a colleague[25] interpreted the data as showing that, if anything, it was the girls in *coeducational* classes who fared better.

Once again, NASSPE misrepresents the main point. In response to an inquiry from us,[26] Rowe commented, "Sax has an extraordinary proclivity to selectively decontextualise my published findings for his own promotional purposes. In fact, I was contacted by the Secretary to the U.S. Congress about the extent to which Sax has correctly cited my findings—to which I responded in the negative."

In the other reports in this section of the NASSPE website, several critics who reviewed the cited studies found problems with their scientific rigor.[27]

NASSPE's category of "before and after" studies consists of good-news stories sourced from the media about schools that have experimented with single-sex classes. One newspaper article[28] cites a study attributed to "researchers at Manchester University." We have been unable to track down this study. Certainly, the School of Education at Manchester University has no record of it.[29]

The third category of "academic studies" contains references to the published work by some well-established researchers but, once again, their work is misrepresented. For example, a 1986 study by researchers Valerie E. Lee and Anthony S. Bryk[30] is cited with no reference to Lee's more recent (1998) assessment of the findings.[31]

Calling single-sex schooling "a quick fix" in the quest for equity, Lee said, "If we're trying to make a better world and we think a sex-equitable world is a better world, I'm not sure separating out girls for education is really the way to do it." She adds that the research on single-sex schooling should not be interpreted as favoring the separation of boys and girls for their education.

NASSPE also distorts the 1990 research of Cornelius Riordan,[32] of Providence College. The group suggests that he has misinterpreted his own results! "Riordan believes that the beneficial effects of single-sex schooling are most impressive for children from underprivileged backgrounds. However, this belief sets him apart from many other researchers in the field, particularly outside the United States." This statement is patently false.

Biological Differences

If NASSPE were simply pointing to good single-sex private schools and saying that public schools could imitate some of their academic practices, there would be no problem. But NASSPE is advocating curricula based on major cognitive differences between boys and girls—similar to those outlined in Leonard Sax's books.

Scientists who find that Sax misrepresents their work, or who see tiny studies being hyped, better studies ignored, and misinformation passed on to teachers around the country often react with a loud gnashing of teeth. Mark Liberman[33] writes: "Leonard Sax has no serious interest in the science of sex differences. He's a politician, making a political argument. For all I know, his political goal— single-sex education—might be a good thing. But he should stop pretending that he's got science on his side, or else he should start paying some minimal attention to what the science actually says."

Lise Eliot (*Pink Brain, Blue Brain*) is even stronger in her critique of Sax and his treatment of "scientific" findings. In her words: "Unfortunately, his presentation of the actual data on single-sex schools suffers from the same sort of cherry-picking as his proclamations about the neurologic differences between boys and girls, showing little effort to fairly weight all the evidence supporting the essential sameness of both sexes or both types of schools."[34]

In addition, the *New York Times Magazine* published in March 2008 a lengthy piece by Elizabeth Weil that was deeply critical of Sax's work.[35] The article describes Liberman's criticism of Sax and also asserts that "many academics and progressives tend to find Sax's views stereotyped and infuriating."

Count us among that group. NASSPE's case is loaded with distortions, misstatements, highly selective coverage of the literature, and denials from the very researchers it quotes. If you're interested in evidence-based science, it's hard to take NASSPE seriously.

Not surprisingly, the NASSPE website prominently displays Sax's book *Why Gender Matters*, in which he maintains that the innate differences between the sexes are such as to require separate education. Now, there are undoubted biological and psychological gender differences, but with the notable exception of the sex organs themselves, few are large and immutable. As we've pointed out again and again in the preceding chapters, on average the great majority of gender differences are small and the overlap between the distributions is large. In short, the differences within each sex are greater than the differences between the sexes. It makes no sense to talk about boys and girls as if they are homogeneous groups that are different enough to warrant separate educational treatment.

Lise Eliot concludes her massive overview of the peer-reviewed literature with a blunt rebuttal of the Sax and Gurian position: "So the argument that boys and girls need different educational experiences because 'their brains are different' is patently absurd. The same goes for arguments based on cognitive abilities, which differ far more within groups of boys or girls than between the average boy and girl"[36]

In addition to anatomical differences, there are undeniable differences between girls and boys, mostly in interpersonal preferences and interests, mostly among older rather than younger children, and mostly massively shaped by boys' and girls' different experiences. Some of these differences advantage girls; others advantage boys. When it comes to preparing children for the adult world they will enter, schools have an important part to play. They can provide each sex with opportunities to gain the skills they might not otherwise develop in our highly sex-segregated world. For example, girls can benefit from opportunities to exert leadership and develop healthy competitiveness; boys can gain from learning to be more cooperative and to take turns. Such differences need to be addressed at school, and that can be done most effectively in a coed environment.

It is of great concern that the unscientific views of Sax and Gurian are increasingly being embraced by teachers and educational policymakers. According to NASSPE,[37] only 11 public schools offered single-gender classrooms in March 2002. By May 2009, at least 542 public schools in 41 states offered single-sex educational options.

Again according to NASSPE, in at least 95 of these schools, students have *all* of their activities—including lunch and all electives—in a single-sex setting. At a time when thoughtful people are arguing for evidence-based policies, the movement toward single-sex schools is particularly alarming.

In our survey of media coverage of the single-sex advocates, we found that most reporters accepted uncritically the theories of such people as Sax and Gurian. For example, on December 9, 2009, CNN's *American Morning*[38] featured a segment on middle schools in Virginia that base their curricula on Sax's theories of brain differences between boys and girls. The CNN story did not note that Sax has an economic interest in promoting such classrooms, since he earns a tidy sum running educator-training programs and conferences to promote sex segregation in public education. And during the piece, the anchor, Kiran Chetry, seemed to be reinforcing the points made by Sax. David Sadker, professor of education at American University, an expert on these issues, got a tiny sound bite that, he said, gave him no time to rebut the flawed science promoted by Sax.

Many of the other stories we examined had similar problems. Reporters presented theories served up by advocates as settled science, often with no opposing point of view. And, if critics were quoted, it was in a throwaway sentence or two late in the story that made them seem to be ill-informed or merely carping.


Separate but Equal?


Another major issue is that the single-sex movement for public schools flies in the face of the constitutionally affirmed principle that separate schools are inherently unequal. The Supreme Court's historic ruling in *Brown v. Board of Education* established that segregating children into separate schools provides different and inherently unequal educational opportunities, and 1972's Title IX mandated equality in education for the sexes. The burden of proof that single-sex schools do not create unequal education should therefore be high; instead, this drastic shift in the way we educate children has been premised on little more than anecdote.

Not only do single-sex public schools violate constitutional principles, but they deprive our children of important learning opportunities and run the very real risk of reinforcing the toxic sex stereotypes that are rampant in our society. Moreover, in a time of scarce resources, it is important to ask whether segregated classes are the way to go. They are expensive, because federal law mandates that any programs set up for one sex must be duplicated for the other. Why not spend the money on programs that we know pay dividends—small classes, good teachers, parent involvement, and enough books, computers, and other educational tools?

After our thorough review of the data, we conclude that the effort to segregate public schools by gender is a misguided effort. Private single-sex schools with excellent students and abundant resources will continue to thrive. The reasons for their success, as we have noted, most likely have little to do with the gender composition of the school and more to do with parents' motivation and superior resources.

Public schools are a different story. They are for all of our children. We do not segregate these schools into classes for Mexicans, Cambodians, African Americans, and whites—even though it could be argued that children might be more comfortable learning with people of their own ethnicity, religion, or culture. And recall that Lise Eliot argues, "Boys and girls can learn a lot from one another: boys coax girls into great physicality, which is good for both body and mind (particularly girls' spatial sense); and girls have a calming effect on boys, helping them focus and settle down to their quieter classroom tasks. So it appears that girls have a moderating effect on a group of boys, while boys have an energizing effect on girls—assuming, of course, that teachers deliberately encourage the two sexes to work together."[39]

In short, the best available research strongly suggests that coeducation should continue to be the standard for our public schools.

# 11 CONCLUSION

On their journey to adulthood, boys and girls often run into different obstacles. But female children increasingly encounter a worrying and growing phenomenon. A culture that is hypersaturated by media has created a problem of crisis proportions, affecting girls at younger and younger ages, in more and more sectors of society.

## The Risks Facing Tween Girls and Boys

The sexualization of girls was examined by a task force of the American Psychological Association in 2007.[1] The exhaustive report that resulted covered television, music videos, music lyrics, movies, magazines, sports media, video games, the Internet, and advertising. According to the report, Nielsen media research found that children watch six hours of television per day, and the Kaiser Foundation found that 51 percent of girls play interactive games on their computers and are surfing on their computers for about an hour a day. What are they doing? Visiting websites, listening to music, and using social media. This exposure to media among youth creates "the potential for massive exposure to portrayals that sexualize women and girls and teach girls that women are sexual objects," says the APA. All the media that were reviewed "emphasize the sexuality of young women to a stunning degree." Music videos are the worst, with some 70 percent of rap and R&B artists including in their songs sexual content degrading to women. An example, from the popular rap artist 50 Cent: "I tell the hos all the time, bitch, get in my car." Commercial video games contain highly sexualized content and few positive female protagonists. Some 46 percent of female characters were presented in a sexual manner.

Studies of magazines aimed at teen girls, the APA reports, "encouraged young women to think of themselves as sexual objects whose lives are not complete unless sexually connected with a man" and constantly emphasized "the need to achieve rigid norms of physical attractiveness through the consumption of products such as cosmetics and fashionable clothing."

Teenagers are the largest group of consumers of movies, but these films offer a stunning lack of female characters. Among 4,000 characters in top-grossing motion pictures, 75 percent were male and 73 percent of speaking roles went to men. The one place where females won out over males was in nudity—females were seen in the nude four times as often as men. The Internet is a growing source of sexual content—fully a quarter of Internet sites are pornographic, and the Kaiser Foundation found that 70 percent of teens had viewed such sites at least once.

Younger and younger girls are being presented in a sexual manner. Miley Cyrus, the wildly popular 16-year-old star of *Hannah Montana*, a show aimed at teen girls, appeared at a music awards show scantily clad and gyrating around a stripper's pole. Britney Spears, a teen singer with a huge girl audience, graduated to senior status by wearing a nude body stocking at the MTV Video Music Awards.

Girls today often display an unhealthy obsession with their body image. They are more and more being victimized by an impossible cultural ideal of thinness perpetuated by the media. Already slender celebrities are routinely "Photoshopped" by magazines to appear thinner than they really are. Fashion models often resemble famine victims. Model Carrie Otis admitted she used cocaine to try and stay a size three. Supermodel Kate Moss also had a cocaine problem and in 2009 was slammed by critics for saying, "Nothing tastes as good as skinny feels."[2] It's no wonder, since the favorite size for Hollywood casting agents, according to reports, is 0–0.

This massive exposure has real consequences for girls. According to the APA report, "Ample evidence indicates that sexualization has negative effects on a variety of domains, including cognitive functioning, physical and mental health, sexuality and attitudes and beliefs." If girls learn that behaving like a sexual object gains approval from society and people whose opinions they respect, they may begin to "self-sexualize"—in fact to become their own worst enemies as far as their health and well-being are concerned

Sexual objectification fractures consciousness. "Chronic attention to physical attractiveness leaves fewer cognitive resources available for other mental and physical activities." In other words, being obsessed with how she looks literally makes a girl dumber. In one experiment, college girls were asked to try on either a swimsuit or a piece of clothing that did not display their bodies and observe themselves. While wearing the garments, they were asked to take a math test. The girls in the swimsuits scored significantly lower than those wearing the outfits that covered more of their bodies. College males who took the same test did not score lower while wearing swim trunks. Other studies show that girls and women who concentrate on what they look like do less well on tests of logical reasoning and spatial skills.

Our culture encourages girls to make decisions that may in fact limit achievement. The APA report states: "Girls may be learning to prioritize certain rewards (male attention) over other rewards (academic accomplishment) thus limiting their future educational and occupational opportunities."

Girls are encouraged by our sexualized media culture to yearn for careers such as fashion model, movie star, rock singer, or pop icon, all of which are very difficult to achieve and available mainly to women who are very young. To the degree that careers in science, math, and technology seem "unsexy," girls may shy away from these areas, even if they have ability. This trend has harmful consequences for these girls' future lives.

Research links sexualization with three of the most common mental health problems of girls and women—depression, eating disorders, and low self-esteem. The connections are not limited by race or class. For both black and white teenage girls, the more they idealized TV images and compared themselves to those images, the more dissatisfied they were with their own bodies.

Perhaps as a result, teens are seeking plastic surgery at an alarming rate. Between 2002 and 2003, the number of girls 18 and younger getting breast implants nearly tripled, from 3,872 to 11,426. In one study, two-thirds of the 16-year-old girls in a suburban high school knew someone who had had cosmetic surgery, and many of the girls interviewed desired it for themselves. The comparison of their own bodies to an impossible standard of beauty creates feelings of shame and anxiety in girls as young as 12 or 13. Girls who consume media images of idealized women often find their own bodies "gross" or revolting.

Teenagers exposed to ads featuring idealized women reported more symptoms of depression, and girls who thought of themselves as sexual objects were more prone to eating disorders, depression, and body shame.

Parents and teachers can contribute to the problem. Parents, peers, and the media all support a "culture of dieting" for girls. Research finds that mothers who are overconcerned about their own weight and appearance and mothers who criticize their daughters about their weight can contribute to eating disorders in girls. One recent longitudinal study of eighth and ninth graders found that mothers routinely engaged in "fat talk" and that girls were surrounded by excessive concerns about appearance and talk of feeling fat. Fewer girls received "body image" messages from their fathers, but those messages that they did receive were jokes, put-downs, and snide comments. African American girls received much more positive feedback from parents about their appearance and had less concern about their weight. But the APA notes, "More African-American women who now gain success in entertainment and the media adhere to the same ideal of extreme thinness as white women," so girls of color may increasingly suffer body-image problems.

Teachers, the APA finds, can also exacerbate the problem. One study showed that teachers disliked girls whose bodies didn't conform to the thin ideal. Boys who were "bulky," however, were liked by teachers. Teachers play "dress up" with girls more than with boys and teachers often encourage girls to play at being sexualized grown-up women, vamping, looking in the mirror, and imitating adult sexy poses.

Another result of the sexualization of girls is the increase of sexual harassment in schools. Boys as well as girls can internalize the idea that girls are supposed to behave like sex objects, and that idea can contribute to such acts as crass sexual jokes, leering, and touching or grabbing at the breasts, buttocks, or vaginas of girls. Research finds that boys exposed to sexualized portrayals of girls may be more prone to commit acts of harassment.

Countering harmful media messages won't be easy, given the torrent of images that kids see each day, but the issue is too vital to ignore.

The APA report says, "Parents can teach girls to value themselves for who they are, rather than how they look" and can also "teach boys to value girls as friends, sisters, and girlfriends, rather than as sexual objects. . . . With the help of the adults in their lives, girls and boys can gain media literacy skills, can learn to resist the message that how girls look is what matters, and can learn how to advocate for themselves."

## Boys Have Issues Too

Boys don't sail through these rough waters untouched, either. We've seen how boys face lowered academic expectations, are told that they naturally lack verbal ability, and experience a "boy culture" that demands that they suppress their emotions, always act tough and in control, and tamp down their natural expressions of empathy. Body image is a charged area for boys as well as for girls. Boys are barraged with literally thousands of images of males whose bodies are buffed and polished to an unnatural degree. Movie stars seem to spend their lives in the gym, and toned males appear constantly on television in ads for exercise equipment. Even the *New York Times*[3] commented on the buffed-up physiques of CNN reporters covering Haiti in 2010:

> Viewers who watched CNN's earthquake coverage were bound to be struck by correspondents who looked a lot less like the usual disheveled examples of those in the profession than like bendable action figures. You could call it the Anderson Cooper effect. Mr. Cooper has rarely missed an opportunity to showcase his physique (as anyone would know if he or she remembers his stripping to a bathing suit to quiz Michael Phelps). But Mr. Cooper isn't the only CNN correspondent with a self-conscious taste for form-fitting charcoal T-shirts, accessorized with a tiny microphone clipped at the neck.
>
> Looking somewhat sheepish about it, a newly sleek Dr. Sanjay Gupta moved through Port-au-Prince wearing a snug gray T-shirt, his hair styled in the obligatory CNN crop. His colleague Jason Carroll, reporting on the aftershock and looking like a guy who had done 20 quick pushups before going on air, wore a T-shirt so snugly revealing it

called into question whether a disaster zone is the place to flaunt one's gym physique.

All this emphasis on the perfect male body is having an effect. According to a study done in Australia,[4] it is estimated that about 45 percent of Western men are unhappy with their bodies to some degree, compared with only 15 percent some 25 years ago.

Boys as young as middle-school age are now conscious of how they are supposed to look. Some 8 million Americans suffer from eating disorders, and conservative estimates suggest that one in 10 of these is male, although some experts put the ratio as high as one in 6. Many more have eating problems that interfere with their lives.[5]

And today, with kids watching as stars in football, baseball, track, and other major sports admit to steroid use, such abuse is increasing among boys. Research[6] suggests that between 7 percent and 11 percent of middle-school boys have used steroids at some point to increase muscle size and tone. Among students in grades 8 through 12 who admitted to using anabolic steroids in a confidential survey, 57 percent said professional athletes influenced their decision to use the drugs and 63 percent said pro athletes influenced their friends' decision to use them. Eighty percent of users—and 35 percent of non-users—said they believed steroids could help them achieve their athletic dreams.

Even more worrying, boys who used steroids said they were willing to take extreme risks to star in sports. The survey found that 65 percent of steroid users versus 6 percent of non-users said they would be willing to use a pill or powder, including dietary supplements, if it guaranteed they would reach their athletic goals *even if it might harm their health*, and 57 percent of users versus 4 percent of non-users said they would take a pill or powder even if it shortened their life.

In 2009, Boston University journalism student Elisa Weiss[7] followed three high school students who easily obtained steroids at a local gym. They were told that if they used the drugs on a start-and-stop cycle, they'd look great and side effects would be minor. The boys noted positive changes in their bodies immediately, but the side effects were hardly minor. They included development of the breasts and shrinking testicles, as well as unexpected outbursts of anger. One of the boys screamed profanely at his mother one night when she asked him to put steaks on the grill for her. "I wasn't even making sense. My mom even asked me if there was something wrong because I was so angry."

## Risky Business?

The proliferation of extreme sports on television and in films may accelerate risk taking in boys. Research[8] finds that "risk-promoting media" lead to an increase in such behavior. And sports programming sends powerful messages to boys, according to a study[9] funded by (among others) the Kaiser Foundation. One of the most powerful of these is that aggression, violence, and injuries are exciting and rewarding.

Boys are five times more likely than girls to watch sports on a regular basis. "According to the sports programming that boys consume most, a real man is strong, tough, aggressive, and above all, a winner in what is still a man's world. To be a winner, he must be willing to compromise his own long-term health by showing guts in the face of danger, by fighting other men when necessary, and by 'playing hurt' when he's injured. He must avoid being soft; he must be the aggressor, both on the 'battlefields' of sports and in his consumption choices. Whether he is playing sports or making choices about which products to purchase, his aggressiveness will win him the ultimate prize: the adoring attention of beautiful women and the admiration of other men."

Such media messages are pushing boys who are prone to risk taking into dangerous territory.[10] Boys more than girls believe they will never be injured, and when they do get hurt, they tend to write off their injuries to "bad luck."

Risk taking is an intrinsic part of many sports, but a hyper-macho image of sports may push boys to try dangerous stunts for which they don't have the experience, and to avoid safety gear because it's just not "cool." Parents, teachers, doctors, and the media need to keep repeating the message that "safety first" isn't wimpy. It just may prevent lifelong crippling injuries or, in the worst-case scenario, early death.

## Same or Different?

Boys and girls may indeed face different challenges as they move toward adulthood. The argument over whether they should be parented and educated in very different ways to better meet those challenges echoes an old argument in American education.

Two currents seem to alternately ebb and flow through the history of U.S. schools—mix kids up or separate them into categories—black-white, gifted-average, boys-girls.

For many years, especially in the South, black children and white children were educated separately, and this situation was believed to be the natural order of things. In 1954 the Supreme Court outlawed de jure (by law) segregation, but many classes in inner cities today remain largely segregated. Some schools "track" kids into separate programs by their IQ scores or their reading and math abilities. As we've seen, the push for segregating classes by gender is being fueled by vocal advocates.

What's best—classrooms full of kids who are very much alike or classrooms filled with children who bring different strengths, life experiences, and talents to the task of learning? Is it better to segregate children so as to maximize homogeneity? Why not separate out the top-performing children from those who are struggling, as many schools do today? Why not put all those who score below a certain cutoff on standardized achievement tests in one class and those who score in the higher range in another? As we have discussed, school achievement is significantly related to race and social class. If we favor homogeneity, perhaps we should advocate for segregating children by these two critical factors. Given how racially and economically segregated our country is, perhaps we are already engaged in that experiment. If so, the results suggest that homogeneity is not a path to closing the big achievement gaps. Given this history, why would anyone think that segregating schools by gender would have a positive effect on academic performance?

While this debate continues, evidence is mounting, as we've shown, that heterogeneity has more beneficial effects than homogeneity does. For example, in business settings, mixed-sex work groups outperform same-sex work groups.[11] Anecdotally, the wildly popular TV series *House* regularly dramatizes positive outcomes when doctors of different specialties and backgrounds work together to determine the diagnoses of patients with complicated cases. The back-and-forth, the differences of opinion, the arguments, the trial-and-error—all increase the likelihood that the team will find the right diagnosis. It is hard to imagine how a team composed of members of just one discipline or race or gender would have similarly positive outcomes.

If you assume that boys and girls learn differently, and should be put into separate classes on the basis of their learning styles, how will they be challenged to think differently, to try different approaches, to break out of their own over-learned approaches to solving problems? Yet the suggestion of creating single-sex schools is not being challenged on the basic principle that heterogeneity trumps homogeneity.

We've seen that boys and girls start out with very small difference in their cognitive abilities, but that over time, the influence of parents, teachers, and messages from society can move children in the direction of stereotypical behavior. This sex segregation might have seemed appropriate 50 years ago, when women were expected to spend their lives in the domestic sphere, not venturing into the workplace. At the same time, the office or factory floor was familiar turf for men, but the nursery or playroom was not. That isn't the world we live in today. In the near future women will outnumber men in the workforce, and today 22 percent of men have wives who out-earn them, compared to 4 percent in 1970.[12]

More and more, men with working wives are doing a larger share of child care and household tasks.[13] Women will be working for much of their lives, and they need to learn to be assertive and comfortable with the idea of competition because these skills are crucial for success in the workplace. Men will be shouldering more and more family responsibilities, and they need to learn to be caring and communicative so that they can be good fathers and husbands—as well as effective managers. Research shows that the best managers combine traits typically thought of as "male" and "female."

Kids, in fact, should be encouraged to move toward the activities and talents traditionally associated with the opposite sex. Lise Eliot endorses the idea of using boys' war play as a vehicle for teaching empathy and negotiating, encouraging children to trade off being the good guys and the bad guys; addressing the same concepts of conflict and danger in other parts of the curriculum, as at story time; offering alternative props for dramatic play that allow boys to be equally powerful but engaged in more humanistic roles (such as firefighters, construction workers, or mountain rescue teams).

Girls, by the same token, can learn to use their verbal skills not only in "relating" to others but also in more assertive ways, such as in debate and in negotiation. While some argue that boys have suffered as a result of Title IX, the law that gave boys and girls a level playing field in resources in sports, we would argue the opposite. Boys have not suffered and girls have become more athletic and physically stronger, are more comfortable with competition, and are enjoying heightened self-esteem by playing sports.

And if today we see girls in school who are focused, achievement-oriented, and performing well academically, we shouldn't immediately cry out that girls have some inborn capacity that boys lack and that boys need separate classrooms to keep up. Boys can learn these skills, and perhaps today's girls offer them a good example.

When sociologist Michael Kimmel interviewed more than 400 white middle-class young men (ages 16 to 26) for his book *Guyland*,[14] he found too many of them reluctant to grow up, having trouble committing to their intimate relationships, work, or social lives. This problem isn't about some inborn "hardwiring," he argues, but about a "guy" culture that exalts video games, sports, and depersonalized sexual relationships while rejecting achievement, hard work, and commitment.

But just as we object vigorously when some urban black kids say that being smart is being "white," we should object just as much to the idea that focusing and achieving just aren't normal "boy" skills. *Guyland* is a place boys don't have to inhabit.

## A Better Path

Harvard's Howard Gardner[15] sees education in a much more holistic way than many of today's gender-difference advocates. As we noted earlier, Gardner believes that children before the age of about 5 or 6 intuitively develop a strong understanding of the world in which they live. But, as they get older, parents, teachers, institutions, and society take over and guide children in certain directions. And kids, eager to please, want to go where these powerful figures guide them. We believe—with Gardner—that the paths laid out for kids need to be broad rather than narrow, encouraging children to develop the entire range of abilities that are within their grasp. Gardner characterizes these multiple intelligences as follows:

1. Linguistic intelligence is the kind of ability exhibited in its fullest form, perhaps, by poets.

2. Logical-mathematical intelligence . . . is logical and mathematical ability, as well as scientific ability.
3. Spatial intelligence is the ability to form a mental model of a spatial world and to be able to maneuver and operate using that model.
4. Musical intelligence.
5. Bodily-kinesthetic intelligence is the ability to solve problems or to fashion products using one's whole body, or parts of the body.
6. Interpersonal intelligence is the ability to understand other people: what motivates them, how they work, how to work cooperatively with them.
7. Intrapersonal intelligence is a seventh kind of intelligence, is a correlative ability, turned inward. It is a capacity to form an accurate, veridical model of oneself and to be able to use that model to operate effectively in life.

## Some Final Thoughts

Don't be taken in by simplistic generalization about "boys" and "girls." Boys differ wildly among themselves, as do girls, making it absurd to talk about the sexes as homogeneous groups. Your daughter is your daughter, with her own skills, abilities, and preferences. She may be no more or less like the girls in her group than like the boys. The same goes for sons. Kids are individuals.

Hard as it may be to tune out these pink-and-blue-box messages, it's important to pay chose attention to *your* child—of whatever sex—and encourage his or her talents and desires.

On the other hand, it's also important to recognize that in our culture boys and girls are exposed to very different stimuli and experiences, and we need to encourage them to venture beyond their ordinary comfort zone.

Crucially, parents, teachers, and others who socialize kids need to examine their own gender stereotypes to be sure that they are not imposing them on children. Without that knowledge, it's hard to keep from reinforcing the old ideas that put kids in straitjackets. Parents and teachers need to remember that children must stretch in order to reach their full potential. As Paul Grobstein,[16] professor of neurobiology at Bryn Mawr College, says, we need to "hold open to individuals the possibility and the opportunity of becoming different from what they are. The goal of education ought to be transformation, perhaps even self-transcendence."

# NOTES

## 2. Brains in Pink and Blue?

1. S. J. Gould, *The Mismeasure of Man* (New York: Norton, 1981).
2. A. Eisenberg, "Women and the Discourse of Science," *Scientific American*, July 1992.
3. B. Pease and A. Pease, *Why Men Don't Listen and Women Can't Read Maps* (New York: Broadway, 2002).
4. M. Gurian, P. Henley, and T. Trueman, *Boys and Girls Learn Differently: A Guide for Teachers* (San Francisco: Jossey-Bass, 2001).
5. L. Sax, *Why Gender Matters: What Parents and Teachers Need to Know About the Emerging Science of Sex Differences* (New York: Doubleday, 2005), 19–21.
6. J. Gray, *Men Are from Mars, Women Are from Venus: A Practical Guide for Improving Communication and Getting What You Want in Your Relationships* (New York: HarperCollins, 1993).
7. M. Liberman, "Neuroscience in the Service of Sexual Stereotypes," *Language Log*, http://itre.cis.upenn.edu/~myl/languagelog/archives/003419.html.

8. D. S. Weisberg, F. C. Keil, J. Goodstein, E. Rawson, and J. R. Gray, "The Seductive Allure of Neuroscience Explanations," *Journal of Cognitive Neuroscience* 20, no. 3 (2008): 470–477.

9. J. Gabriel, *The Truth About Girls and Boys*, http://www.brainconnection.com/content/91_1. 2001.

10. M. D. Devous, D. Altuna, N. Furl, W. Cooper, G. Gabbert, W. T. Ngai, et al., "Maturation of Speech and Language Functional Neuroanatomy in Pediatric Normal Controls," *Journal of Speech, Language, and Hearing Research* 49, no. 4 (2006): 856–866.

11. R. K. Lenroot, N. Gogtay, D. K. Greenstein, E. M. Wells, G. L. Wallace, L. S. Clasen, et al., "Sexual Dimorphism of Brain Developmental Trajectories During Childhood and Adolescence," *NeuroImage* 36 (2007): 1065–1073.

12. NationalAssociationforSingleSexPublicEducation.http://www.singlesexschools.org/research-brain.htm.

13. R. K. Lenroot, personal communication, August 3, 2009.

14. V. J. Schmithorst and S. K. Holland, "Sex Differences in the Development of Neuroanatomical Functional Connectivity Underlying Intelligence Found Using Bayesian Connectivity Analysis," *NeuroImage* 35, no. 1 (2007): 406–419.

15. R. J. Haier, R. E. Jung, R. A. Yeo, K. Head, and M. T. Alkire, "The Neuroanatomy of General Intelligence: Sex Matters," *NeuroImage* 25, no. 1 (2005): 320–327.

## 3. More Pink and Blue

1. S. Baron-Cohen, *The Essential Difference: The Truth About the Male and Female Brain* (New York: Basic Books, 2003).

2. E. S. Spelke, "Sex Differences in Intrinsic Aptitude for Mathematics and Science? A Critical Review," *American Psychologist* 60, no. 9 (2005): 950–958.

3. "Girls Prefer Dolls (to Blocks and Toys)," *Parents* magazine, June 2007.

4. "The Difference Between Boys and Girls," *Parents* magazine, March 2006.

5. C. D. de Lacoste-Utamsing and R. L. Holloway, "Sexual Dimorphism in the Human Corpus Callosum," *Science* 216, no. 4553 (1982): 1431–1432.

6. C. Gorman and M. J. Nash, "Sizing Up the Sexes," *Time*, January 20, 1992.

7. "The New Science of the Brain: Why Men and Women Think Differently," *Newsweek*, March 27, 1995.

8. A. Fausto-Sterling, *Sexing the Body: Gender Politics and the Construction of Sexuality* (New York: Basic Books, 2000).

9. K. M. Bishop and D. Wahlsten, "Sex Differences in the Human Corpus Callosum: Myth or Reality?" *Neuroscience and Biobehavioral Review* 21, no. 5 (1997): 581–601.

10. Ibid.

11. L. Eliot, *Pink Brain, Blue Brain* (New York: Houghton Mifflin Harcourt, 2009).

12. "The Difference Between Boys and Girls," *Parents* magazine, March 2006.

13. L. Brizendine, *The Female Brain* (New York: Broadway Books, 2006).

14. S. Orbach and J. Schwartz, "Playing the Gender Game: Why Are Little Boys Slugs and Snails While Little Girls Are All Things Nice?" *Guardian*, June 11, 1997.

15. R. A. Fabes and N. Eisenberg, "Meta-analyses of Age and Sex Differences in Children's and Adults' Prosocial Behavior," in W. Damon, ed., *Handbook of Child Psychology*, 5th ed., vol. 3, *Social, Emotional, and Personality Development*, ed. N. Eisenberg (New York: Wiley, 1998).

16. J. B. Miller, *Toward a New Psychology of Women* (Boston: Beacon Press, 1976).

17. S. E. Snodgrass, "Further Effects of Role Versus Gender on Interpersonal Sensitivity," *Journal of Personality and Social Psychology* 62, no. 1 (1992): 154–158.

18. T. Canli, J. E. Desmond, Z. Zhao, and J. D. Gabrieli, "Sex Differences in the Neural Basis of Emotional Memories," *Proceedings of the National Academy of Sciences* 99 (2002): 10789–10794.

19. S. Connor, "Men Aren't Heartless, It's All in the Mind," *Independent*, London, July 23, 2002.

20. M. Dowd, "What's a Modern Girl to Do?" *New York Times Magazine*, October 30, 2005, 50.

21. D. Brooks, "Is Chemistry Destiny?" *New York Times*, September 17, 2006.

22. L. Brizendine, *The Female Brain* (New York: Broadway Books, 2006).

23. R. M. Henig, "Taking Play Seriously," *New York Times*, February 17, 2008.

24. M. A. Strauss, "Physical Assaults by Women Partners: A Major Social Problem," in M. R. Walsh, ed., *Women, Men, and Gender: Ongoing Debates*, 210–221 (New Haven, Conn.: Yale University Press, 1997).

25. N. R. Crick, M. A. Bigbee, and C. Howes, "Gender Differences in Children's Normative Beliefs About Aggression: How Do I Hurt Thee?" *Child Development* 67 (1996): 1003–1014.

26. K. Osterman, K. Bjorkqvist, M. J. Dirsti, A. K. Lagerspetz, S. F. Landau, A. Fraczek, and G. V. Caprara, "Is Indirect Aggression Typical of Females? Gender Differences in Aggressiveness in 11- to 12-Year-Old Children," *Aggressive Behavior* 14 (1998): 403–414.

27. M. Gurian, *The Wonder of Boys: What Parents, Mentors, and Educators Can Do to Shape Boys Into Exceptional Men* (Toronto: Penguin, 2006).

28. M. Gurian, *The Wonder of Girls: Understanding the Hidden Nature of Our Daughters* (New York: Pocket Books, 2002).

29. S. Rhoads, *Taking Sex Differences Seriously* (New York: Encounter Books, 2004).

30. J. Edwards, "Science? Psychology? Religion?" Review of M. Gurian, *The Wonder of Girls: Understanding the Hidden Nature of Our Daughters*, Culture Cartel.com, February 7, 2002.

31. G. Swainson, "Girls Not Wired for Science, Author Claims," *Toronto Star*, January 10, 2002.

32. "They're Too Smart for These Guys," *Chicago Sun Times*, December 15, 2005.

33. "Are Men Insecure or Are They Merely Intimidated?" *Toronto Star*, January 7, 2005.

34. J. Schwartz, "Glass Ceilings at Altar As Well As Boardroom," *New York Times*, December 14, 2004.

35. "Too Smart to Marry?" *Atlantic*, April 2005.

36. M. Dowd, "Men Just Want Mommy," *New York Times*, January 13, 2005.

37. M. D. Taylor, C. L. Hart, G. D. Smith, L. J. Whalley, D. J. Hole, V. Wilson, et al., "Childhood IQ and Marriage by Mid-Life: The Scottish Mental Survey 1932 and the Midspan Studies," *Personality and Individual Differences* 38, no. 7 (2005): 1621–1630.

38. S. L. Brown and B. P. Lewis, "Relational Dominance and Mate-Selection Criteria: Evidence That Males Attend to Female Dominance," *Evolution and Human Behavior* 25 (2004): 406–415.

39. G. K. Baruch, C. Rivers, and R. C. Barnett, *Lifeprints: New Patterns of Love and Work for Today's Women* (New York: New American Library, 1983).

40. V. K. Oppenheimer, "Women's Employment and the Gain to Marriage: The Specialization and Trading Models," *Annual Review of Sociology* 23 (1997): 431–453; H. Boushey, *Are Mothers Really Leaving the Workplace?* (Washington, D.C.: Council on Contemporary Families and the Center for Economic and Policy Research, 2006).

41. Boushey, *Are Mothers Really Leaving the Workplace?*

42. J. S. Hyde, J. D. DeLamater, and A. M. Durik, "Sexuality and the Dual-Earner Couple, Part II: Beyond the Baby Years," *Journal of Sex Research* 38, no. 1 (2001): 10–23.

43. A. C. Huston and S. R. Aronson, "Mothers' Time with Infant and Time in Employment as Predictors of Mother-Child Relationships and Children's Early Development," *Child Development* 76, no. 2 (2005): 467.

44. M. F. Belenky, B. M. Clinchy, N. R. Goldberger, and J. M. Tarule, *Women's Ways of Knowing: The Development of Self, Voice, and Mind* (New York: Basic Books, 1986).

45. V. Gornick, "Woman as Outsider," in V. Gornick and B. K. Moran, eds., *Woman in Sexist Society*, 137–144 (New York: Basic Books, 1971).

46. A. Eisenberg, "Women and the Discourse of Science," *Scientific American*, July 1992.

47. D. F. Halpern, *Sex Differences in Cognitive Abilities* (Mahwah, N.J.: Earlbaum, 2000).

48. D. F. Halpern, personal communication, August 17, 2009.

49. A. H. Eagly, M. C. Johannesen-Schmidt, M. van Engen, and L. Marloes, "Transformational, Transactional, and Laissez-faire Leadership Styles: A Meta-Analysis Comparing Women and Men," *Psychological Bulletin* 129, no. 4 (2003): 569–591.

50. R. J. Haier, R. E. Jung, R. A. Yeo, K. Head, and M. T. Alkire, "The Neuroanatomy of General Intelligence: Sex Matters," *NeuroImage* 25, no. 1 (2005): 320–327.

## 4. Math Wars

1. D. Blum, "Solving for XX: What Science Can (and Can't) Tell Larry Summers About the Difference Between Men and Women," *Boston Globe*, January 23, 2005.

2. K. Parker, "Larry Summers and the Thought Police," *Real Clear Politics*, 2007.

3. S. Quinn, "The Misguided Mathematics of Equating Women and Men," *Washington Post*, February 19, 2005.

4. G. Will, "Damned Lies and . . ." *Newsweek*, March 29, 1999.

5. "Summertime Blues," *Financial Times*, February 9, 2005.

6. C. P. Benbow and J. C. Stanley, "Sex Differences in Mathematical Ability: Fact or Artifact?" *Science* 210 (1980): 1262–1264.

7. "Are Boys Better at Math?" *New York Times*, December 7, 1980.

8. "The Gender Factor in Math," *Time*, December 15, 1980.

9. A. Fausto-Sterling, *Myths of Gender: Biological Theories About Men and Women* (New York: Basic Books, 1985).

10. L. Fox, "Sex Differences Among the Mathematically Precocious," *Science* 224 (1984): 224.

11. V. Valian, *Why So Slow? The Advancement of Women* (Cambridge, Mass.: MIT Press, 1999).

12. G. Swainson, "Girls Not Wired for Science, Author Claims," *Toronto Star*, January 10, 2002.

13. A. Hermann, "Girls, It Seems, Will Be Girls," *Chicago Tribune*, February 17, 2002.

14. E. S. Spelke, "Sex Differences in Intrinsic Aptitude for Mathematics and Science? A Critical Review," *American Psychologist* 60, no. 9 (2005): 950–958.

15. A. Gopnik, "Your Baby Is Smarter Than You Think," *New York Times*, August 16, 2009.

16. L. Schulz and E. B. Bonawitz, "Serious Fun: Preschoolers Engage in More Exploratory Play When Evidence Is Confounded," *Developmental Psychology* 43, no. 4 (2007): 1045–1050.

17. J. S. Hyde and J. E. Mertz, "Gender, Culture, and Mathematics Performance," *Proceedings of the National Academy of Sciences, USA* 106, no. 22 (2009): 8801–8807.

18. Ibid..

19. Ibid.

20. D. F. Halpern, C. P. Benbow, D. C. Geary, R. C. Gur, J. S. Hyde, and M. A. Gernsbacher, "The Science of Sex Differences in Science and Mathematics," *Psychological Science in the Public Interest* 8 (2007): 1–51.

21. Ibid.

22. Hyde and Mertz, "Gender, Culture, and Mathematics Performance."

23. J. S. Hyde, S. M. Lindberg, M. C. Linn, A. B. Ellis, and C. C. Williams, "Gender Similarities Characterize Math Performance," *Science* 321 (2008): 494–495.

24. S. Mead, "The Truth About Boys and Girls," *Education Sector*, June 2006.
25. Halpern et al., "The Science of Sex Differences in Science and Mathematics."
26. M. Carpenter, "Why Girls Score Low on SAT's Baffling," *Pittsburgh Post-Gazette*, August 27, 2003.
27. J. S. Hyde, E. Fennema, and S. J. Lamon, "Gender Differences in Mathematics Performance: A Meta-Analysis," *Psychological Bulletin* 107, no. 2 (1990): 139–155.
28. Hyde and Mertz, "Gender, Culture, and Mathematics Performance."
29. D. F. Halpern, Sex *Differences In Cognitive Abilities* (Mahwah, N.J.: Earlbaum, 2000).
30. A. Moir and D. Jessel, *Brain Sex: The Real Difference Between Men and Women* (New York: Viking, 1997).
31. S. Rhoads, *Taking Sex Differences Seriously* (New York: Encounter Books, 2004).
32. L. Brizendine, *The Female Brain* (New York: Broadway Books, 2006).
33. E. Leahey and G. Guo, "Gender Differences in Mathematical Trajectories," *Social Forces* 80, no. 2 (2001): 713–732.
34. D. Blum, *Sex on the Brain: The Biological Differences Between Men and Women* (New York: Viking, 1997).
35. L. J. Harris, "Sex Differences in Spatial Ability: Possible Environmental, Genetic, and Neurological Factors," in M. Kinsbourne, ed., *Asymmetrical Function of the Brain*, 405–522 (New York: Cambridge University Press, 1978).
36. E. E. Maccoby and C. N. Jacklin, *The Psychology of Sex Differences* (Stanford, Calif.: Stanford University Press, 1974.
37. H. Lips, A. Myers, and N. Colwill, "Sex Differences in Ability: Do Men and Women Have Different Strengths and Weaknesses?" in H. Lips and N. Colwill, eds., *Psychology of Sex Difference*, 145–173 (Englewood Cliffs, N.J.: Prentice-Hall, 1978).
38. B. Pease and A. Pease, *Why Men Don't Listen and Women Can't Read Maps* (New York: Broadway, 2002).

39. R. Compton, *Old Bones Shatter New Myths: Biology as Destiny* (Sociobiology Study Group, Science for the People, Cambridge, Mass., 1984).

40. D. Harraway, *Primate Visions: Gender, Race, and Nature in the World of Modern Science* (New York: Routledge, 1989).

41. D. Voyer, S. Voyer, and B. M. Philip, "Magnitude of Sex Differences in Spatial Abilities: A Meta-analysis and Consideration of Critical Variables," *Psychological Bulletin* 117, no. 2 (1995): 250–270.

42. P. J. Caplan, G. M. MacPherson, and P. Tobin, "Do Sex-Related Differences in Spatial Abilities Exist? A Multilevel Critique with New Data," *American Psychologist* 40, no. 7 (1985): 786–799.

43. C. Dowling, *The Frailty Myth: Redefining the Physical Potential of Women and Girls* (New York: Random House, 2000).

44. J. Feng, I. Spence, and J. Pratt, "Playing an Action Video Game Reduces Gender Differences in Spatial Cognition," *Psychological Science* 18 (2007): 850–855.

45. L. M. Marulis, L. L. Lui, C. M. Warren, D. H. Uttal, and N. S. Newcombe, "Effects of Training or Experience on Spatial Cognition in Children and Adults: A Meta-analysis" (paper presented at the annual meeting of the American Educational Research Association, Chicago, April 2007).

46. M. B. Casey, R. L. Nuttall, E. Pezaris, and C. P. Benbow, "The Influence of Spatial Ability on Gender Differences in Mathematics College Entrance Test Scores Across Diverse Samples," *Developmental Psychology* 31 (1995): 697–705.

47. S. Sorby, "Educational Research in Developing 3-D Spatial Skills for Engineering Students," *International Journal of Science Education* 31 (2009): 459–480.

48. J. S. Eccles, B. Barber, and D. Jozefowicz, "Linking Gender to Educational, Occupational, and Recreational Choices: Applying the Eccles et al. Model of Achievement-Related Choices," in W. B. Swann, J. H. Langlois, and L. A. Gilbert, eds., *Sexism and Stereotypes in Modern Society: The Gender Science of Janet Taylor Spence*,

153–191 (Washington, D.C.: American Psychological Association, 1999).

49. M. M. Bleeker and J. E. Jacobs, "Achievement in Math and Science: Do Mothers' Beliefs Matter 12 Years Later?" *Journal of Educational Psychology* 96, no. 1 (2004): 97–109.

50. K. Crowley, M. A. Callanan, H. R. Tenenbaum, and E. Allen, "Parents Explain More Often to Boys Than to Girls During Shared Scientific Thinking," *Psychological Science* 12 (2001): 258–261.

51. J. Tiedemann, "Parents' Gender Stereotypes and Teachers' Beliefs as Predictors of Children's Concept of Their Mathematical Ability in Elementary School," *Journal of Educational Psychology* 92, no. 1 (2001): 144–151; J. E. Jacobs and J. S. Eccles, "The Impact of Mothers' Gender-Role Stereotypic Beliefs on Mothers' and Children's Ability Perceptions," *Journal of Personality and Social Psychology* 63, no. 6 (1992): 932–944.

52. Jacobs and Eccles, "The Impact of Mothers' Gender-Role Stereotypic Beliefs on Mothers' and Children's Ability Perceptions."

53. E. H. Luchins, "Women and the Pursuit of a Career in Mathematics," *Christian Science Monitor*, May 17, 1981.

54. S. L. Boswell, "The Influence of Sex-Role Stereotyping on Women's Attitudes and Achievement in Mathematics," in S. F. Chipman, L. R. Brush, and D. M. Wilson, eds., *Women and Mathematics: Balancing the Equation*, 91 (New York: Erlbaum, 1985).

55. Ibid.

56. Ibid.

57. T, Schmader, M. Johns, and M. Barquissau, "The Costs of Accepting Gender Differences: The Role of Stereotype Endorsement in Women's Experience in the Math Domain," *Sex Roles* 50, nos. 11–12 (2004): 835–850.

58. C. M. Steele, "A Threat in the Air: How Stereotypes Shape the Identities and Performance of Women and African Americans," *American Psychologist* 52 (1997): 613–629.

59. S. M. Campbell and M. L. Collaer, "Stereotype Threat and Gender

Differences in Performance on a Novel Visuospatial Task," *Psychology of Women Quarterly* 33 (2009): 437–444.

60. E. Spelke, "Edge: The Science of Gender and Science." www.edge. org/3rd_culture/debate05/debate05_index.htm, May 16, 2005.

61. C. Wennerås and A. Wold, "Nepotism and Sexism in Peer-Review," *Nature* 387, no. 22 (1997): 341–343.

62. S. L. Beilock, E. A. Gunderson, G. Ramirez, and S. C. Levine, "Female Teachers' Math Anxiety Affects Girls' Math Achievement," *Proceedings of the National Academy of Sciences, USA* 107, no. 5 (2010): 1060–1063.

63. L. Smith-Doerr, *Women's Work: Gender Equality vs. Hierarchy in the Life Sciences* (Boulder, Col.: Lynne Rienner Publishers, 2004).

64. "A Study on the Status of Women Faculty in Science at MIT," *MIT Faculty Newsletter* 11, no. 4 (March 1999).

65. "Teens Prepared for Math, Science Careers, Yet Lack Mentors," *MIT News*, January 7, 2009.

66. D. Milgram, "Gender Differences in Learning Style Specific to Science, Technology, Engineering, and Math" (July 24, 2007). Retrieved September 17, 2009, from http://ezinearticles. com/?G ender-Differences-In-Learning-Style-Specific-To-Science,-Technology,-Engineering-And-Math—Stem&id=658953.

67. A. Fisher, J. Margolis, and F. Miller, "Undergraduate Women in Computer Science: Experience, Motivation, and Culture," *ACM SIGCSE Bulletin* 29, no. 1 (1997): 106–110.

## 5. Word Play

1. M. S. Kimmel, "The Contemporary Crisis of Masculinity in Historical Perspective," in Harry Brod, ed., *The Making of Masculinities*, 121–153 (Winchester, Mass.: Allen and Unwin, 1987).

2. T. Jan, "Schoolboy's Bias Suit Argues System Is Favoring Girls," *Boston Globe*, January 26, 2006.

3. P. Tyre, "The Trouble with Boys," *Newsweek*, January 30, 2006.

4. R. Whitmire, "Boy Trouble," *New Republic*, January 23, 2006.

5. S. Mead, "The Evidence Suggests Otherwise: The Truth About Boys and Girls," *Education Sector, Research and Reports*, June 27, 2007.

6. C. B. Swanson, *Caps, Gowns, and Games: High School Graduates and NCLB* (Washington, D.C.: Urban Institute, 2003).

7. I. Khatiwada and A. Sum, *Gender Differences in High School Graduation Rates and College Enrollment Rates of Graduates from Boston Public High Schools in Recent Years: Findings of the Follow-up Surveys for the Classes of 1999, 2000, and 2001 and Agenda for Future Research* (Boston: Boston Private Industry Council and Boston Public Schools, 2002).

8. J. P. Greene and G. Forster, *Public High School Graduation and College Readiness Rates in the United States* (New York: Manhattan Institute for Policy Research, 2003).

9. R. Lowry, "Biology's Revenge: Christina Hoff Sommers Was Right," *National Review Online*, January 24, 2006.

10. "Boys Learn Better in Motion," *Atlanta Journal-Constitution*, October 27, 2006.

11. *Hartford Courant*, August 15, 2006, http://creativedestruction.wordpress.com/2006/08/15/more-boy-crisis-the-connecticut-mastery-test/.

12. D. Brooks, "The Education of Robert Kennedy," *New York Times*, November 26, 2006.

13. Mead, "The Evidence Suggests Otherwise."

14. J. S. Hyde and M. C. Linn, "Gender Differences in Verbal Ability: A Meta-analysis,". *Psychological Bulletin* 104 (1988): 53–69.

15. D. F. Halpern, *Sex Differences in Cognitive Abilities* (Mahwah, N.J.: Erlbaum, 2000).

16. M. Kimmel, "A War Against Boys?" *Dissent*, Fall 2006.

17. V. E. Lee, "Sexism in Single-Sex and Coeducational Independent Secondary School Classrooms," *Sociology of Education* 67, no. 2 (1994): 92–120.

18. M. Conlin, "The New Gender Gap: From Kindergarten to Grad School, Boys Are Becoming the Second Sex," *Business Week*, May 26, 2003, 74.

19. C. H. Sommers, *The War Against Boys: How Misguided Feminism Is Harming Our Young Men* (New York: Simon and Schuster, 2000).

20. N. Perry, "Gender Gap: Progress or Problem?" *Seattle Times*, October 3, 2005.

21. J. Wapner, "Scientist at Work: He Counts Your Words (Even Those Pronouns)," *New York Times*, October 14, 2008.

22. S. Lutchmaya, S. Baron-Cohen, and P. Raggatt, "Foetal Testosterone and Vocabulary Size in 18- and 24-Month-Old Infants," *Infant Behavior and Development* 24, no. 4 (2001): 418–424.

23. J. T. Manning, *Digit Ratio: A Pointer to Fertility, Behavior, and Health* (Newark, N.J.: Rutgers University Press, 2002).

24. M. W. Clearfield, "Sex Differences in Mothers' Speech and Play Behavior with 6-, 9-, and 14-Month-Old Infants," *Sex Roles* 54, nos. 1–2 (2006).

25. V. Flynn and E. F. Masur, "Characteristics of Maternal Verbal Style: Responsiveness and Directiveness in Two Natural Contexts," *Journal of Child Language* 34, no. 3 (2007): 519–543.

26. O. Z. Weizman and C. E. Snow, "Lexical Input as Related to Children's Vocabulary Acquisition: Effects of Sophisticated Exposure and Support for Meaning," *Developmental Psychology* 37, no. 2 (2001): 265–279.

27. C. Leaper, K. J. Anderson, and P. Sanders, "Moderators of Gender Effects on Parents' Talk to Their Children: A Meta-analysis," *Developmental Psychology* 34, no. 1 (1998): 3–27.

28. P. Greenfield, J. Reilly, C. Leaper, and N. Baker, "The Structural and Functional Status of Single-Word Utterances and Their Relationship to Early Multi-Word Speech," in M. D. Barrett, ed., *Children's Single-Word Speech*, 233–267 (Chichester, UK: Wiley, 1985).

29. A. C. Huston, "Sex-Typing," in P. H. Mussen and E. M. Hetherington, eds., *Handbook of Child Psychology*, vol. 4, *Socialization*,

*Personality, and Social Development*, 387–467 (New York: Wiley, 1983).

30. J. B. Gleason, "Sex Differences in the Language of Children and Parents," in O. Garnica and M. King, eds., *Language, Children, and Society*, 149–157 (Oxford, UK: Pergamon, 1979).

31. M. Clearfield and N. Nelson, "Sex Differences in Mothers' Speech and Play Behavior with 6-, 9-, and 14-Month-Old Infants," *Sex Roles* 54, nos. 1–2 (2006): 127–137.

32. M. J. Galsworthy, G. Dionne, P. S. Dale, and R. Plomin, "Sex Differences in Early Verbal and Non-verbal Cognitive Development," *Developmental Science* 3, no. 2 (2000): 206–215.

33. R. Weis and B. C. Cerankosky, "Effects of Video-Game Ownership on Young Boys' Academic and Behavioral Functioning: A Randomized, Controlled Study," *Psychological Science OnlineFirst*, February 18, 2010.

34. L. Sax, *Why Gender Matters: What Parents and Teachers Need to Know About the Emerging Science of Sex Differences* (New York: Broadway Books, 2005).

35 D. Brooks, "Mind Over Muscle," *New York Times*; October 16, 2005; H. Brod, *The Making of Masculinities: The New Men's Studies* (New York: Routledge, 1987).

## 6. Toy Choice

1. B. E. Hort, "Children's Use of Metaphorical Cues in Gender-Typing Novel and Familiar Objects" (paper presented at the Society for Research in Child Development meeting, Ann Arbor, 1993); B. E. Hort, M. D. Leinbach, and B. I. Fagot, "Metaphorically Gendered Traits and the Gender-Typing of Toys" (paper presented at the 1992 Western Psychological Association Conference, Phoenix); B. E. Hort, M. D. Leinbach, and B. Fagot, "Summary of Gender-Typing Studies for SRCD Talk" (paper presented at 1993 Society for Research on Child Development meeting, Ann Arbor).

2. T. Raag and C. L. Rackliff, "Preschoolers' Awareness of Social Expectations of Gender: Relationships to Toy Choices," *Sex Roles* 38, nos. 9/10 (1998): 685–700.

3. M. Kimmel, "About a Boy," *Vassar Alumnae Quarterly*, Winter 2003.

4. K. Benezra, "Toys Unfair," *Brandweek* 36 (February 13, 1995): 20–24.

5. L. M. Brown, S. Lamb, and M. Tappan, *Packaging Boyhood: Saving Our Sons from Superheroes, Slackers, and Other Media Stereotypes* (New York: St. Martin's Press, 2009).

6. T. Bartlett, "The Puzzle of Boys," *Chronicle Review*, November 22, 2009; New-York-auto-show-polly-wheels-gives-young-girls- their-own-line (April 4, 2007), www.autoblog.com/.

7. New-York-auto-show-polly-wheels-gives-young-girls-their-own-line; R. Flass, "Desperate Dolls: Barbie, Bratz Face Weak Demand," *Advertising Age*, October 31, 2005.

8. R. Flass, "Desperate Dolls."

9. D. Levin, and J. Kilbourne, "So Sexy, So Soon: The New Sexualized Childhood and What We Can Do About It," *Forum Network*, http://forumnetwork.org/lecture/so-sexy-so-soon-new-sexualized-childhood.

10. G. MacNaughton, *Shaping Early Childhood* (Columbus, Ohio: McGraw-Hill Education, 2003).

11. L. M. Brown and S. Lamb, "Let's Go: No Makeover for Dora!" www.ipetitions.com/petition/Dora_Makeover/.

12. C. Brown, "Woman Warrior," *Newsweek*, June 8, 1998.

13. M. E. Williams, "The Princess and the Frog Is Disney Royalty," Salon.com, November 24, 2009.

## 7. The More Aggressive Sex?

1. C. Frey, and S. Hoppe-Graff, "Serious and Playful Aggression in Brazilian Girls and Boys," *Sex Roles* 30, nos. 3–4 (1994): 249–269.

2. B. Thorne, *Gender Play: Girls and Boys in School* (New Brunswick, N.J.: Rutgers University Press, 1993).

3. R. L. Munroe, R. Hulefeld, J. M. Rodgers, D. L. Tomeo, and S. K. Yamazaki, "Aggression Among Children in Four Cultures," *Cross-Cultural Research* 34, no. 1 (2000): 3–25.

4. M. Gurian, P. Henley, and T. Trueman, *Boys and Girls Learn Differently: A Guide for Teachers* (San Francisco: Jossey-Bass, 2001).

5. J. A. DiPietro, "Rough and Tumble Play: A Function of Gender," *Developmental Psychology* 17, no. 1 (1981): 50–58.

6. Ibid.

7. A. Bandura, D. Ross, and S. A. Ross, "Transmission of Aggression Through Imitation of Aggressive Models," *Journal of Abnormal and Social Psychology* 63 (1961): 575–582.

8. J. R. Lightdale and D. A. Prentice, "Rethinking Sex Differences in Aggression: Aggressive Behavior in the Absence of Social Roles," *Personality and Social Psychology Bulletin* 20, no. 1 (1994): 34–44.

9. S. Biddulph, *Raising Boys: Why Boys Are Different—and How to Help Them Become Happy and Well-Balanced Men* (Berkeley, Calif.: Celestial Arts, 2008).

10. A. P. Humphreys and P. K. Smith, "Rough and Tumble, Friendship, and Dominance in Schoolchildren: Evidence for Continuity and Change with Age," *Child Development* 58, no. 1 (1987): 201–212.

11. T. Reed and M. Brown, "The Expression of Care in the Rough and Tumble Play of Boys," *Journal of Research in Childhood Education* 15, no. 1 (2000): 104–116.

12. M. Tannock, "Rough and Tumble Play: An Investigation of the Perceptions of Educators and Young Children," *Early Childhood Education Journal* 35, no. 4 (2008): 357–361.

13. C. N. Jacklin, "Methodological Issues in the Study of Sex-Related Differences," *Developmental Review* 1, no. 3 (1981): 266–273.

14. P. Chesler, *Woman's Inhumanity to Woman* (Chicago: Lawrence Hill Books, 2009).

15. V. K. Burbank, "Cross-cultural Perspectives on Aggression in Women and Girls: An Introduction," *Sex Roles* 30, nos. 3/4 (1994): 169–176.

16. M. A. Straus, "Physical Assaults by Women Partners: A Major Social Problem," in M. R. Walsh, ed., *Women, Men, and Gender: Ongoing Debates*, 210–222 (New Haven, Conn.: Yale University Press, 1997); M. A. Straus and R. J. Gelles, *Physical Violence in American Families* (New Brunswick, N.J.: Transaction Publishers, 1990).

17. R. P. Rohner, "Sex Differences in Aggression: Phylogenetic and Enculturation Perspectives," *Ethos* 4, no. 1 (1976): 57–72.

18. K. Osterman, K. Björkqvist, K. M. J. Lagerspetz, A. Kaukiainen, S. F. Landau, A. Fraczek, et al., "Cross-cultural Evidence of Female Indirect Aggression," *Aggressive Behavior* 24 (1998): 1–8.

19. Ibid.

20. Ibid.

21. K. Björkqvist, "Sex Differences in Physical, Verbal, and Indirect Aggression: A Review of Recent Research," *Sex Roles* 30, nos. 3–4 (1994): 177–188.

22. J. Garbarino, *See Jane Hit: Why Girls Are Growing More Violent and What We Can Do About It* (New York: Penguin, 2006).

23. E. R. Mondschein, K. E. Adolph, and C. S. Tamis-LeMonda, "Gender Bias in Mothers' Expectations About Infant Crawling," *Journal of Experimental Child Psychology* 77 (2000): 304—316; M. R. Walsh, *Women, Men, and Gender: Ongoing Debates* (New Haven, Conn.: Yale University Press, 1997); "From Trinidad and Tobago" (Yale Department of Economics, Labor and Population Workshop, September 11, 2009).

24. "From Trinidad and Tobago."

## 8. Caring

1. Sloan Wilson, *The Man in the Gray Flannel Suit* (New York: Four Walls Eight Windows, 1953).

2. J. H. Pleck, "The Theory of Male Sex-Role Identity: Its Rise and Fall, 1936 to the Present," in H. Brod., ed., *The Making of Masculinities: New Men's Studies*, 21–38 (New York: Allen and Unwin, 1987).

3. N. Chodorow, *The Reproduction of Mothering: Psychoanalysis and the Sociology of Gender* (Berkeley: University of California Press, 1978).

4. D. Blankenhorn, *Fatherless America: Confronting Our Most Urgent Social Problem* (New York: Basic Books, 1995).

5. D. W. Winnicott, *The Child, the Family, and the Outside World* (New York: Addison-Wesley, 1987).

6. R. H. Passman, "Attachments to Inanimate Objects: Are Children Who Have Security Blankets Insecure?" *Journal of Consulting and Clinical Psychology* 55, no. 6 (1987): 825–830; R. H. Passman and P. Wiesberg, "Mothers and Blankets as Agents for Promoting Play and Exploration by Young Children in a Novel Environment: The Effects of Social and Nonsocial Attachment Objects," *Developmental Psychology* 11, no. 2 (1975): 170–177.

7. M. S. Ainsworth, "Infant-Mother Attachment," *American Psychologist* 34, no. 10 (1979): 932–937.

8. See www.google.com/imgres?imgurl=http://www.gogohamsters.org.

9. G. Melson, personal communication, August 7, 2009.

10. B. B. Whiting, *Children of Six Cultures: A Psycho-Cultural Analysis* (Cambridge, Mass.: Harvard University Press, 1975); Melson, personal communication, August 7, 2009.

11. Melson, personal communication, August 7, 2009.

12. Ibid.

13. J. Blakemore, "Children's Nurturant Interactions with Their Infant Siblings: An Exploration of Gender Differences and Maternal Socialization," *Sex Roles* 22 (1990): 43–57.

14. Ibid.

15. W. Pollack, *Real Boys: Rescuing Our Sons from the Myths of Boyhood* (New York: Holt, 1997).

16. F. Crosby, *Juggling: The Unexpected Advantages of Balancing Career and Home for Women and Their Families* (New York: Free Press, 1991).

17. J. Gray, *Men Are from Mars, Women Are from Venus: A Practical Guide for Improving Communication and Getting What You Want in Your Relationships* (New York: HarperCollins, 1993).

18. B. J. Risman, and D. Johnson-Sumerford, "Doing It Fairly: A Study of Postgender Marriages," *Journal of Marriage and the Family* 60 (1998): 23–40.

19. L. B. Silverstein and C. F. Auerbach, "Deconstructing the Essential Father," *American Psychologist* 54, no. 6 (1999): 397–407.

20. E. Galinsky, K. Aumann, and J. T. Bond, *2008 National Study of the Changing Workforce* (New York: Family Work Institute, 2009).

21. J. F. Sandberg and S. L. Hofferth, *Changes in Children's Time with Parents, U.S. 1981–1997* (Population Studies Center Research Report No. 01–475, Institute for Social Research, University of Michigan, 2001).

22. *Life's Work: Generational Attitudes Towards Work and Life Integration* (Radcliffe Public Policy Center, Radcliffe Institute for Advanced Study, Cambridge, Mass., 2000).

23. J. Snarey, *How Fathers Care for the Next Generation: A Four-Decade Study* (Cambridge, Mass.: Harvard University Press, 1993).

24. Galinsky, Aumann, and Bond, *2008 National Study of the Changing Workforce*.

## 9. The Ideal Classroom

1. F. G. Graves and L. S. Kaufmann, <http://nwlc.blogs.com/womens-take/2007/04/about_the_blogg.html#fatima>.

2. S. Adcox, "S.C. at Forefront of Single-Gender Classes," *Boston Globe*, October 1, 2007.

3. A. Neal, *The Case Against Sex-Segregated Classrooms* (ACLU of Alabama Research on Women and Education, Birmingham, 2009).

4. M. Liberman, "Liberman on Sax on Liberman on Hearing," http://languagelg.ldc.upenn.edu/nll/?p=171 (2008).

5. M. Gurian, P. Henley, and T. Trueman, *Boys and Girls Learn Differently: A Guide for Teachers* (San Francisco: Jossey-Bass, 2001), 30.

6. J. Large, "A Recipe for Growing Good Men," *Seattle Times*, May 14, 2009.

7. Cited in E. Weil, "Teaching Boys and Girls Separately," *New York Times Magazine*, March 2, 2008.

8. Ibid.

9. Ibid.

10. M. Galley, "Research: Boys to Men," www.edweek.org/login.html?source=http://www.edweek.org/ew/articles/2002/01/23/19boys.h21.html&destination=http://www.edweek.org/ew/articles/2002/01/23/19boys.h21.html&levelId=2100.

11. D. T. Caceci, "Anatomy and Physiology of the Eye," http://education.vetmed.vt.edu/curriculum/VM8054/EYE/EYEDEMO.HTM (retrieved May 4, 2009).

12. Ibid.

13. L. Sax, *Why Gender Matters. What Parents and Teachers Need to Know About the Emerging Science of Sex Differences* (New York: Doubleday, 2005), 21.

14. Caceci, "Anatomy and Physiology of the Eye."

15. M. Gurian and A. C. Ballew, *The Boys and Girls Learn Differently Action Guide for Teachers* (San Francisco: Jossey-Bass, 2003).

16. C. H. Hillman, S. M. Buck, J. R. Themanson, M. B. Pontifex, and D. M. Castelli, "Aerobic Fitness and Cognitive Development: Event-Related Brain Potential and Task Performance Indices of Executive Control in Preadolescent Children," *Developmental Psychology* 45, no. 1 (2009): 114–129.

17. "Physical Activity May Strengthen Children's Ability to Pay Attention," *Science Daily*, April 1, 2009, www. Science daily.com/ releases /2009/03/090331183800.htm.
18. Hillman, personal communication, April 1, 2009.
19. Cited in Weil, "Teaching Boys and Girls Separately."
20. N. Angier, "A Hit in School, Maggots and All," *New York Times*, May 12, 2009.
21. S. Rubins, personal communication, May 19, 2009.
22. Hillman et al., "Aerobic Fitness and Cognitive Development."
23. Ibid.
24. B. Thorne, *Gender Play: Girls and Boys in School* (New Brunswick, N.J.: Rutgers University Press, 1993).
25. C. H. Sommers, *The War Against Boys: How Misguided Feminism Is Harming Our Young Men* (New York: Simon and Schuster, 2000).
26. M. Gurian, *The Wonder of Boys: What Parents, Mentors, and Educators Can Do to Shape Boys Into Exceptional Men* (New York: Tarcher, 1997).
27. T. Bartlett, "The Puzzle of Boys," *Chronicle of Higher Education*, November 22, 2009.
28. "Education: Learning Styles Debunked," *Science Daily*, December 17, 2009, www.sciencedaily.com/releases/2009/12/091216162356.htm.
29. H. Pashler, M. McDaniel, D. Rohrer, and R. Bjork, "Learning Styles: Concepts and Evidence," *Psychological Science in the Public Interest* 9, no. 3 (2009): 105–119.
30. R. S. Bigler, "Good Morning, Boys and Girls," www.tolerance.org/ magazine/number-28-fall-2005/good-morning-boys-and-girls (Fall 2005).

## 10. Single-Sex Education, Pros and Cons

1. See www.americaspromise.org.
2. Colin Powell, www.americaspromise.org.

3. National Coalition of Girls' Schools Alumnae Survey (1999), Goodman Research Group, Cambridge, Mass.

4. F. Mael, A. Alonso, D. Gibson, K. Rogers, and M. Smith, *Single-Sex Versus Coeducational Schooling: A Systematic Review* (Washington, D.C.: American Institutes for Research, U.S. Department of Education, Office of Planning, Evaluation, and Policy Development, 2005).

5. R. Hotakainen, "Single Sex Schools Are Separate but Not Always Equal," *Minneapolis Star Tribune*, June 9, 2002.

6. A. Datnow, L. Hubbard, and E. Woody, *Is Single Gender Schooling Viable in the Public Sector? Lessons from California's Pilot Program*, Final Report (New York: Ford Foundation and Chicago: Spencer Foundation 2001).

7. S. Morse, ed., *Separated by Sex: A Critical Look at Single-Sex Education for Girls* (Washington, D.C.: American Association of University Women Educational Foundation, 1998).

8. J. Shepherd, "Girls Make Boys Worse at English," *Guardian*, April 21, 2009.

9. S. Proud, "Girl Power? An Analysis of Peer Effects Using Exogenous Changes in the Gender Make-up of the Peer Group" (working paper 08/186, University of Bristol, England, 2008).

10. A. Smithers and P. Robinson, *The Paradox of Single Sex and Coeducational Schooling* (Buckingham UK: Carmichael Press University of Buckingham, 2006).

11. J. S. Hyde, S. M. Lindberg, M. C. Linn, A. B. Ellis, and C. C. Williams, "Gender Similarities Characterize Math Performance," *Science* 321, no. 5888 (2008): 494–495.

12. Smithers and Robinson, *The Paradox of Single Sex and Co-educational Schooling*.

13. *Selecting an Independent School: The Benefits of the Coeducational Experience*, www.ridleycollege.com/ftpimages/180/download/download_group4184_id171639.pdf (2006).

14. K. J. Rowe, "The Effects of Class Type on Student Achievement, Confidence, and Participation in Mathematics," *Australian Journal of Education* 32 (1988): 180–202.

15. G. Able, cited in Smithers and Robinson, *The Paradox of Single Sex and Co-educational Schooling.*

16. Smithers and Robinson, *The Paradox of Single Sex and Co-educational Schooling.*

17. See www.singlesexschools.org/schools-schools.htm.

18. L. Sax, *Why Gender Matters: What Parents and Teachers Need to Know About the Emerging Science of Sex Differences* (New York: Broadway Books, 2005).

19. J. Nicholson, A. Gelpi, S. Young, and E. Sulzby, "Influences of Gender and Open-ended Software on First Graders' Collaborative Composing Activities on Computers," *Journal of Computing in Childhood Education* 9 (1998): 3–42.

20. J. Lunnon, "Samantha and Goliath," *Times Educational Supplement*, July 14, 2006.

21. See www.singlesexschools.org/evidence.html.

22. M. Warrington and M. Younger, "Single-Sex Classes and Equal Opportunities for Girls and Boys: Perspectives Through Time from a Mixed Comprehensive School in England," *Oxford Review of Education* 27, no. 3 (2001): 339–356.

23. Smithers and Robinson, *The Paradox of Single Sex and Co-educational Schooling.*

24. C. Dean, "Inspectors Say Girls' Schools Are the Best," *Times Educational Supplement*, October 9, 1998.

25. H. W. Marsh and K. J. Rowe, "The Effects of Single-Sex and Mixed-Sex Mathematics Classes Within a Co-educational School: A Reanalysis and a Comment," *Australian Journal of Education* 40 (1996): 147–162.

26. K. J. Rowe, personal communication, March 12, 2009.

27. A. Paulson, "Move to Single-Sex Classes Fans Debate," *Christian Science Monitor*, October 26, 2006.

28. J. Henry, "Help for the Boys Helps the Girls," *Times Educational Supplement*, June 1, 2001.

29. Smithers and Robinson, *The Paradox of Single Sex and Co-educational Schooling.*

30. V. E. Lee and A. S. Bryk, "Effects of Single-Sex Secondary Schools on Student Achievement and Attitudes," *Journal of Educational Psychology* 78, no. 5 (1986): 394.

31. V. E. Lee, *Separated by Sex: A Critical Look at Single Sex Education for Girls* (Washington, D.C.: American Association of University Women, 1998).

32. C. Riordan, *Girls and Boys in School: Together or Separate* (New York: Teachers College Press, 1990).

33. Liberman, quoted in E. Weil, "Teaching Boys and Girls Separately," *New York Times Magazine*, March 2, 2008.

34. L. Eliot, *Pink Brain, Blue Brain* (New York: Houghton Mifflin Harcourt, 2009).

35. Weil, "Teaching Boys and Girls Separately."

36. Eliot, *Pink Brain, Blue Brain*.

37. NAASPE, www.singlesexschools.org/home.php.

38. "Tell CNN to Stop Promoting Sex Segregation in Public Schools," http://majorityspeaks.wordpress.com/2009/12/11/tell-cnn-to-stop-promoting-sex-segregation-in-public-schools/.

39. Eliot, *Pink Brain, Blue Brain*.

## 11. Conclusion

1. *Report of the APA Task Force on the Sexualization of Girls* (Washington, D.C.: American Psychological Association, 2007).

2. "Kate Moss Sparks Uproar Over 'Feeling Thin,'" *Improper Fashion*, November 19, 2009, www.theimproper.com/fashion/?p=44.

3. G. Trebay, "Disaster Coverage Without Having to Roll Up the Sleeves," *New York Times*, January 21, 2010.

4. D. Witmer, "Do Boys Have Body Image Issues Too?" http://parentingteens.about.com/od/bodyimage/f/boys_bodyimage.htm.

5. L. Pappano, "Boys and Eating Disorders," *Good Housekeeping*, January 27, 2010.

6. L. Smolak, S. K. Murnen, and J. K. Thompson, "Sociocultural Influences and Muscle Building in Adolescent Boys," *Psychology of Men and Masculinity* 6, no. 4 (2005): 227–239.

7. E. Weiss, "Guys, Steroids, and the Muscular Ideal," *Mantra Magazine*, April 2009.

8. P. Fischer, S. Guter, and D. Frey, "The Effects of Risk-Promoting Media on Inclinations Toward Risk Taking," *Basic and Applied Social Psychology* 30, no. 3 (2008): 230–240.

9. M. Messner, D. Hunt, M. Dunbar, P. Chen, J. Lapp, and P. Miller, *Boys to Men: Sports Media: Messages About Masculinity*, 2001, www.aafla.org/9arr/ResearchReports/boystomen.pdf.

10. B. A. Morrongiello and H. Rennie, "Why Do Boys Engage in More Risk Taking Than Girls? The Role of Attributions, Beliefs, and Risk Appraisals," *Journal of Pediatric Psychology* 23, no. 1 (1998): 33–43.

11. D. A. Thomas, "Diversity as Strategy," *Harvard Business Review* 82 (2004): 99–108.

12. R. Fry and D. Cohn, *New Economics of Marriage: The Rise of Wives* (Washington, D.C.: Pew Research Center, 2010).

13. T. Bond, C. T. Thompson, E. Galinsky, and D. Prottas, *The 2002 National Study of the Changing Workforce: Executive Summary* (New York: Families and Work Institute, 2002).

14. M. Kimmel, *Guyland: The Perilous World Where Boys Become Men* (New York: HarperCollins, 2009).

15. H. Gardner, *Multiple Intelligences* (New York: Basic Books, 1993).

16. J. Gabriel, "The Truth About Boys and Girls," *Brain Connection*, July 2001, www.brainconnection.com/content/91_4.

# INDEX

**DATE DUE**

| | | | |
|---|---|---|---|
| | | | |
| | | | |
| | | | |
| | | | |
| | | | |
| | | | |
| | | | |
| | | | |
| | | | |
| | | | |
| | | | |
| | | | |
| | | | |
| | | | |
| | | | |
| | | | |
| | | | |

Demco